The Social
Change Model

SEATTLEU.

SERVE LOCAL

>>> CENTER FOR <<<
COMMUNITY ENGAGEMENT

The Social
Change Model

Facilitating Leadership Development

Kristan Cilente **Skendall**

Daniel T. **Ostick**

Susan R. **Komives**

Wendy **Wagner**

and **Associates**

JB JOSSEY-BASS™
A Wiley Brand

Published by Jossey-Bass

A Wiley Brand

One Montgomery Street, Suite 1000, San Francisco, CA 94104-4594—www.josseybass.com

Jossey-Bass books and products are available through most bookstores. To contact Jossey-Bass directly call our Customer Care Department within the U.S. at 800-956-7739, outside the U.S. at 317-572-3986, or fax 317-572-4002.

Wiley publishes in a variety of print and electronic formats and by print-on-demand. Some material included with standard print versions of this book may not be included in e-books or in print-on-demand. If this book refers to media such as a CD or DVD that is not included in the version you purchased, you may download this material at http://booksupport.wiley.com. For more information about Wiley products, visit www.wiley.com.

Library of Congress Cataloging-in-Publication Data

Names: Skendall, Kristan C., editor. | Ostick, Daniel T., editor. |
    Komives, Susan R., editor. | Wagner, Wendy, editor.
Title: The social change model : facilitating leadership development /
    [edited by] Kristan C. Skendall, Daniel T. Ostick, Susan R. Komives,
    Wendy Wagner.
Description: San Francisco, CA : Jossey-Bass, 2017.
Identifiers: LCCN 2016044789 (print) | LCCN 2016054908 (ebook) | ISBN
    9781119242437 (pbk.) | ISBN 9781119242710 (pdf) | ISBN 9781119242703 (epub)
Subjects: LCSH: Educational leadership—Handbooks, manuals, etc.
Classification: LCC LB2806 .S594 2017 (print) | LCC LB2806 (ebook) |
    DDC 371.2—dc23
LC record available at https://lccn.loc.gov/2016044789

Cover image: Wiley
Cover design: © mythja /Getty Images, Inc.

Printed in the United States of America
FIRST EDITION

PB Printing   10 9 8 7 6 5 4 3 2 1

To the entire Ensemble who envisioned leadership to make a better world and to all leadership educators who advance that vision through their leadership training, education, development, scholarship, and research!

CONTENTS

ACKNOWLEDGMENTS

The development of this facilitation guide was a true work of collaboration. Many individuals offered advice, support, input, and content to help craft all of the materials and activities contained in this book.

Kristan and Daniel are grateful to Susan and Wendy for their work as editors of *Leadership for a Better World* (2nd edition), which built the framework upon which this book is based. Their leadership expertise and commitment to social change resulted in a powerful product for leadership educators, one which we are all proud to build upon. The individual authors in *Leadership for a Better World* (2nd edition) also provided the raw materials to guide the development of each activity within this guide. Special thanks also goes out to the original members of the Ensemble, without whom the Social Change Model would not exist.

Additional thanks goes out to the authors of each of the chapters within this book as well. These leadership educators and scholars from across the United States have contributed their best activities, their best thinking, and years of leadership experience.

Matt Cooney
Ben Correia-Harker
Matt Creasy
Sherry Early
Chris Esparza
Matt Johnson
Mika Karikari
Danielle Kleist
Steve Mencarini
Suresh Mudragada
Darren Pierre

José Riera
Melissa Rocco
Kristen Rupert
Rian Satterwhite
Jordyn Wright

We are particularly thankful to our stellar editor Alison Knowles and the entire team at Jossey-Bass. Their guidance and careful review gave us both the direction and support needed to tackle challenges head-on. Alison's support of leadership education to advance the field is greatly appreciated. We are also thankful to Craig Slack at the National Clearinghouse for Leadership Programs (NCLP) for his assistance with permissions for the guide and constant support of our work. We are grateful to Natasha Chapman, Krystal Clark, Matt Johnson, Ramsey Jabaji, Julie Owen, and Tom Segar for their review of this book, especially the activities in each chapter. Their helpful feedback enhanced this volume tremendously.

Our thanks also go to our families and friends who offered continual encouragement, and to our university departments and supervisors for all of their support.

INTRODUCTION

Leadership for a Better World (2nd edition) describes and explores the Social Change Model (SCM) of Leadership Development as a purposeful, collaborative, values-based process that results in positive social change (Komives, Wagner, & Associates, 2017). The SCM was created specifically for college students who seek to lead in a more socially responsible way and who want to learn to work effectively with others to create social change over their lifetimes (Higher Education Research Institute, HERI, 1996). The creators of the SCM were interested in developing a process of leadership that begins with a personal commitment and self-understanding that is transformed through working collaboratively with others, and meant to serve a larger, societal need or purpose.

The chapters in *Leadership for a Better World* (2nd edition) have been intentionally sequenced into sections, to build upon recent research related to the developmental sequencing of the SCM (Dugan et al., 2014). These sections move from individual values to group values to societal values, and conclude with an examination of how these values work together to accomplish change.

Understanding the Social Change Model (SCM) of Leadership Development This section describes the Social Change Model (SCM), introduces the concept of change and socially responsible leadership, and sets the context for this approach to collaborative, values-based leadership.

Individual Values The second section examines leadership development from the individual perspective or level, and what personal qualities should be fostered. The three values explored are *Consciousness of Self*, *Congruence*, and *Commitment*.

Group Values The third section examines leadership development as a relational process, and how individuals work together toward change. The three values explored are *Collaboration*, *Common Purpose*, and *Controversy with Civility*.

Societal and Community Values The fourth section examines leadership development in relation to the rights of membership and the responsibilities individuals and groups have to serve others and address shared needs and problems. The value explored is *Citizenship*.

On Change The last section examines how all of the values work together to accomplish change, including how change occurs, how people engage with change, and how individuals and groups can implement the Social Change Model in their own leadership.

> ## This Book

The purpose of *The Social Change Model: Facilitating Leadership Development* is to provide active learning strategies for organizing a workshop, activity, or academic course around *Leadership for a Better World* (2nd edition) and the Social Change Model in general. Learning activities in this guide will support curricular and co-curricular applications of the Social Change Model. Each chapter in *Leadership for a Better World* (2nd edition) is addressed here through activities to help participants understand, appreciate, and apply the values of the Social Change Model. The rubrics included in *Leadership for a Better World* (2nd edition) serve as excellent resources for facilitator and participant use.

Introductory chapters introduce the Social Change Model (Chapter One), provide insight into teaching leadership (Chapter Two), and introduce case studies as a pedagogy for exploring the model more deeply (Chapter Three). Subsequent chapters contain summaries of key concepts from the corresponding chapter from *Leadership for a Better World* (2nd edition) and activities, as well as additional readings, resources, and discussion questions. Depending on space constraints, time limitations, and group size, each activity may be modified to accommodate the group and purpose of the activity. These activities can be presented at a basic level or deconstructed for additional complexity, and can also be adjusted for the developmental readiness of the participants. This book provides many resources for facilitators and educators, though many more exist in print and online. It is imperative that leadership educators remain thoughtful consumers of information as access to resources continually expands.

The materials contained in *The Social Change Model: Facilitating Leadership Development* have been designed by some of the best leadership educators in the field of higher education who were chosen based on their content knowledge and pedagogical strengths. We think you will enjoy learning from them.

We know you will discover interesting and useful activities throughout this guide to help you engage with students about socially responsible leadership and social change.

Kristan Cilente Skendall

Daniel T. Ostick

Susan R. Komives

Wendy Wagner

References

Dugan, J.P., Bohle, C.W., Woolker, L.R., & Cooney, M.A. (2014). The role of social perspective-taking in developing students' leadership capacities. *Journal of Student Affairs Research and Practice, 51*, 1–15. doi:10.1515/jsarp-2014-0001

Higher Education Research Institute (HERI). (1996). A social change model of leadership development (Version III). Los Angeles, CA: University of California Los Angeles, Higher Education Research Institute. Retrieved from www.heri.ucla.edu/PDFs/pubs/ASocialChangeModelofLeadershipDevelopment.pdf

Komives, S.R., Wagner, W., & Associates. (2017). *Leadership for a better world: Understanding the social change model of leadership development* (2nd ed.). San Francisco, CA: Jossey-Bass.

Chapter 1

▼

The Social Change Model of Leadership Development for Leadership Educators

Kristan Cilente Skendall & Daniel T. Ostick

◇

"Leadership is the way we invade our future."

SUSAN KOMIVES

Leadership educators shape the future through their work. The Social Change Model (SCM) of Leadership Development is a tool to help in that process. Designed as a complement to *Leadership for a Better World* (2nd Edition) and for use in applications of the SCM in retreats and workshops, this book, *The Social Change Model: Facilitating Leadership Development*, provides resources for leadership educators to teach the SCM via interactive, scaffolded learning exercises. The activities and resources provided are designed to work in curricular and co-curricular settings, and are appropriate for those new to the SCM and those with a more advanced understanding of leadership studies.

> Brief History of Leadership

The concept of leadership has evolved a lot over the past 2,000 years. There are hundreds of definitions of leadership (Rost, 1991) and new approaches emerge regularly. Early approaches to leadership were leader-centric and focused on an individual's traits (Bass, 1990; Rost, 1991). The Great Man Theory approached leadership as a genetic quality, passed down over generations. The early 1900s brought a new approach to leadership, one focused on inherent traits, rather than bloodlines. While trait theory is still present, our understanding of leadership has expanded exponentially over the past 100 years. Mid-twentieth century scholars researched behavioral approaches to leadership giving way to situational and contingency theories of leadership (Bass, 1990; Rost, 1991).

Although trait theory, situational leadership, and behavioral approaches to leadership are still in use today, a more relational, post-industrial approach to leadership emerged at the end of the twentieth century. *Leadership*, a pivotal book by J. M. Burns (1978), signaled a shift from a leader-centric view of leadership to a process-oriented approach to leadership. Burns highlighted the importance of ethics and the relationship between people in leadership positions, with transactional leadership being a quid pro quo model more akin to management, and transforming leadership the foundation for leadership that is most used today.

The Social Change Model of Leadership Development

The postindustrial paradigm (Rost, 1991) that emerged in the 1980s influenced current approaches to leadership, particularly the Relational Leadership Model (Komives, Lucas, & McMahon, 2013) and the Social Change Model (SCM) of Leadership Development (Higher Education Research Institute [HERI], 1996). Astin and Leland's (1991) hallmark study of women involved in social change movements set the groundwork for the Social Change Model's creation. Shortly after *Women of Influence, Women of Vision* (Astin & Leland, 1991) was published, an Eisenhower grant was made available to college and university researchers interested in leadership development. Alexander and Helen Astin served as the co-principal investigators for a grant to understand student leadership and social change. They brought together the top scholars on leadership with student affairs professionals engaged in student leadership work.

This research team called themselves "the Ensemble" and they adopted an approach to their work that would mirror the product they developed. This team was comprised of many musicians, which was an important influence on the development of the SCM as it informed how the group came together. Like a jazz ensemble, the SCM Ensemble team built off of the work of one another in an organic manner, and fostered innovation and creativity in the process of developing the SCM.

Once the Ensemble had a working approach to their new model, they hosted a summit to examine and tune the model with representatives from several professional organizations whose missions focused on leadership. In 1996, Helen Astin published a foundational article about the SCM in *About Campus* and the Social Change Model Guidebook (HERI, 1996) was released. Over the past 20 years, "the social change model of leadership development and the seven C's of social change have played a prominent role in shaping the curricula and formats of undergraduate leadership education initiatives in colleges and universities throughout the country" (Kezar, Carducci, & Contreras-McGavin, 2006, p. 142).

Assumptions of the SCM

The Social Change Model is an approach to leadership that is both process-oriented and outcome-oriented, approaching "leadership as a purposeful, collaborative, values-based process that results in positive social change" (Komives, Wagner, & Associates, 2017, p. 19). Although social change is the ultimate goal of the SCM, the socially responsible process of leadership it outlines is equally as important. The underlying assumptions of the SCM are as follows:

- *Leadership is socially responsible; it impacts change on behalf of others.*
- *Leadership is collaborative.*
- *Leadership is a process, not a position.*
- *Leadership is inclusive and accessible to all people.*

- *Leadership is values-based.*
- *Community involvement/service is a powerful vehicle for leadership.*
  (Astin 1996; Bonous-Hammarth, 2001; HERI, 1996; Komives, Wagner, & Associates, 2016)

These assumptions are the foundation for the Social Change Model, which consists of three levels of development and eight core values. At the Individual level, the SCM values are *Consciousness of Self*, *Congruence*, and *Commitment*. Next, at the Group level, the SCM values include *Common Purpose*, *Collaboration*, and *Controversy with Civility*. The final level, Society/ Community, consists of the value of *Citizenship*. The final value of the SCM is *Change*. Each of these C values is laid out in its own chapter in both *Leadership for a Better World* (Komives, Wagner, & Associates, 2017) and in this volume. Change is split into two chapters, with an overview of Change processes as well as a chapter on *Social Change*. See Figure 1.1 for a visual representation of the SCM and Chapter Four for a greater overview of the SCM.

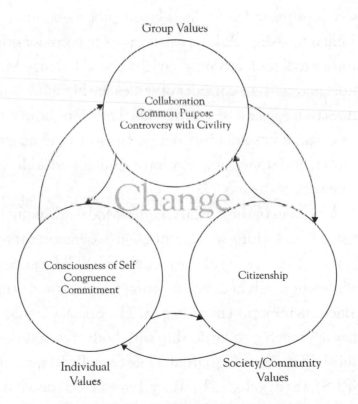

Figure 1.1   The Social Change Model of Leadership Development

> Limitations and Benefits of the SCM

The Social Change Model has been used for twenty years on and off college campuses. While it is highly beneficial, it is not without critique. The Social Change Model was created and conceived as a tool for use in college student leadership contexts, so the initial concept of the SCM and its related research has focused primarily on undergraduate college students. It is also an aspirational model of leadership, one that sometimes exists in contrast to organizational realities. This disconnect does not invalidate the Social Change Model, but is important to acknowledge and understand as a leadership educator. Helping participants understand this disconnect and work toward an aspirational approach to leadership across sectors is an important learning objective of the Social Change Model.

Another noted critique of the Social Change Model is related to what can be perceived as missing C values, such as creativity, culture, curiosity, and caring. The Social Change Model is not a perfect approach to leadership, and as a values-based, process-oriented model, it cannot be all-encompassing. Asking participants to consider other missing values is another tool for learning about the Social Change Model. Leadership educators may wish to consider other leadership models to flesh out important values that speak to their individual missions or institutional priorities. The original Ensemble encouraged educators to adapt the model for their context, and some campuses have emphasized additional values in the framework of the model.

Critiques of the Social Change Model are useful to leadership educators engaged in teaching and learning. Just as important to understanding the SCM are the benefits of the model. The SCM can be used for individuals at different levels of developmental readiness and is more complex than a surface examination may suggest. The Social Change Model is one of only a few approaches to leadership with both an assessment tool and research published in refereed journals. The Socially Responsible Leadership Scale (SRLS) was developed by Tracy Tyree (1998) and has since been adapted to increase validity and reliability of the instrument (Appel-Silbaugh, 2005;

Dugan, Komives, & Associates, 2006). The SRLS is available through the National Clearinghouse for Leadership Programs (www.nclp.umd.edu) and can be used by individuals or groups as an assessment tool for each of the C values (thestamp.umd.edu/srls).

The SCM also serves as the foundational theory undergirding the Multi-Institutional Study of Leadership (MSL) and measured by the SRLS. The MSL is an international research study designed originally by John Dugan and Susan Komives in 2005 to measure the values of the SCM. The MSL has conducted six administrations of the instrument, in 2006, 2009, 2010, 2011, 2012, and 2015. Many refereed publications, reports, theses, and dissertations have studied the data from iterations of the study. More than 250 institutions and 300,000 students have participated in the MSL since its inception. Information related to research findings is included throughout this book and is available online at http://leadershipstudy.net. The Social Change Model is one approach to leadership, and this book provides educators with tools to facilitate learning in a variety of contexts.

References

Appel-Silbaugh, C. (2005). *SRLS revised: The revision of SRLS*. College Park, MD: National Clearinghouse for Leadership Programs.

Astin, H. S., & Leland, C. (1991). *Women of influence, women of vision: A cross-generational study of leaders and social change*. San Francisco, CA: Jossey-Bass.

Astin, H. S. (1996). Leadership for social change. *About Campus, 1*(3), 4–10. doi: 10.1002/abc.6190010302

Bass, B. M. (1990). *Bass & Stogdill's handbook of leadership: Theory, research, & management applications* (3rd ed.). New York, NY: Free Press.

Bonous-Hammarth, M. (2001). Developing social change agents: Leadership development for the 1990s and beyond. In C. L. Outcault, S. K. Faris, & K. N. McMahon (Eds.), *Developing non-hierarchical leadership on campus: Case studies and best practices in higher education* (pp. 34–39). Westport, CT: Greenwood.

Burns, J. M. (1978). *Leadership*. New York, NY: Harper & Row.

Dugan, J. P., Komives, S. R., & Associates. (2006). *Multi-institutional study of leadership: A guidebook for participating campuses.* College Park, MD: National Clearinghouse for Leadership Programs.

Higher Education Research Institute. (HERI) (1996). *A social change model of leadership development (Version III).* Los Angeles, CA: University of California Los Angeles, Higher Education Research Institute.

Kezar, A. J., Carducci, R., & Contreras-McGavin, M. (2006). Rethinking the "L" word in higher education: The revolution in research on leadership. *ASHE Higher Education Report, 31* (6). San Francisco, CA: Jossey-Bass.

Komives, S. R., Lucas, N., & McMahon, T. R. (2013). *Exploring leadership: For college students who want to make a difference* (3rd ed.). San Francisco, CA: Jossey-Bass.

Komives, S. R., Wagner, W., & Associates. (2017). *Leadership for a better world* (2nd Ed.). San Francisco, CA: Jossey-Bass.

Rost, J. C. (1991). *Leadership for the twenty-first century.* Westport, CT: Praeger.

Tyree, T. M. (1998). Designing an instrument to measure the socially responsible leadership using the social change model of leadership development. *Dissertation Abstracts International, 59*(06), 1945. (AAT 9836493)

Kristan Cilente Skendall serves as the Associate Director of the Gemstone Honors Program in the Honors College at the University of Maryland, College Park, where she earned her doctorate in college student personnel. Previously, she worked at Georgetown University, the University of Arizona, and the U.S. Department of Education. Kristan has served as a co-lead facilitator with the LeaderShape Institute, has taught numerous leadership courses, has presented at dozens of national and international conferences, was a member of the Multi-Institutional Study of Leadership Research Team, and served as the coordinator for the National Clearinghouse for Leadership Programs.

Daniel T. Ostick serves as the Assistant Director for Student and Staff Development in the Department of Resident Life at the University of Maryland. where he earned his doctorate in college student personnel. Previously, he worked in Assessment and as the Coordinator for Leadership Curriculum Development and Academic Partnerships in the Adele H. Stamp Student Union-Center for Campus Life at the University of Maryland. Daniel regularly teaches coursework on leadership theory and global leadership, and has published articles and chapters on the Social Change Model (SCM) of Leadership Development, diversity and leadership, and LGBT issues and leadership.

Chapter 2

˅

Teaching Leadership

Matthew R. Johnson

◇

❯ Setting the Context

Teaching leadership, at first blush, seems relatively straightforward: Explore various leadership theories that have evolved over the last two centuries; create a learning environment that balances theoretical content and experiential learning; and push participants to articulate their leadership philosophy amidst the deluge of leadership models, theories, and characteristics. But, upon deeper reflection, this seemingly manageable task becomes intensely more complex.

Consider first that participants in your learning environment have been sold a script that leadership can be learned in a short period. They have been told that mastering leadership can be accomplished in six steps, by embracing nine essential characteristics, or that doing one specific thing will make them better at practicing leadership if they purchase this particular book, attend this unique seminar, or even click a link on a webpage. Educators might also realize that the kind of leadership they are teaching, like that contained in this text, is at odds with the leadership being played out in front of participants in their institutions, communities, states, or countries. Leadership educators are right to realize that to be effective, they must consider the contexts in which participants have formed their current understanding and values related to leadership. Participants are not empty vessels awaiting the fulfillment of knowledge. They have knowledge, and in the case of leadership, they have a lot of knowledge and perhaps even experience—even if it is simplistic, ill-suited for their purposes, or inadequate to create a better world.

› Exploring Participants' Understanding of Leadership

If participants are not blank slates when it comes to leadership, then it behooves educators to understand participants' current understanding of leadership at the beginning of a course or workshop. Asking participants to define leadership on a notecard, map leadership concepts on the board, tell their leadership story, draw their view of leadership, or respond to a series of statements about leadership are all examples of strategies to gauge participants' current understanding of leadership.

To begin to unpack their participants' socialization of leadership messages, facilitators could ask participants to keep a cultural audit of leadership messages they receive over a 24-hour period. They could ask participants to note and describe both implicit and explicit messages they receive about leadership, and then share their observations with the group at the next meeting. These activities can elicit vital information to educators, which will allow them to meet participants where they currently are in their understanding. These glimpses provide an important starting point for thinking about leadership, while the overall learning objectives or outcomes serve as the hopeful endpoint. The following section, "Knowing, Being, Doing," provides guidance on creating learning outcomes.

› Knowing, Being, Doing

When crafting learning outcomes for a leadership course or workshop, educators should be attuned to the three dimensions of development, which include the cognitive, intrapersonal, and interpersonal, commonly referred to as *knowing*, *being*, and *doing* (Komives, Lucas, & McMahon, 2013). Vella (2002) argues that for true learning to occur, shifts must happen in all three of these areas. Simply gaining knowledge, for instance, falls short of transformational learning.

- *Knowing*—what participants know, which includes theories, models, and research related to leadership as well as application of theories and models, particularly those associated with socially responsible leadership.
- *Being*—how participants are, which includes attitudes, dispositions, and values. Participants wrestle with how to engage in socially responsible leadership effectively.
- *Doing*—what participants do, which includes interpersonal skills and abilities related to leadership. Participants learn to act in ways that are congruent with socially responsible leadership.

These three dimensions are important to consider when crafting learning outcomes or simply determining what facilitators hope participants will gain as a result of the course or workshop. When teaching leadership, it is important to incorporate outcomes from all three dimensions.

> Shaping the Learning Environment

Once learning outcomes are established, attention turns to how to create an environment where participants can achieve these learning outcomes. While many aspects can influence a learning environment, negotiating the culture with students and paying attention to the physical layout of the learning space can be essential for creating a positive learning environment.

Negotiating learning space culture

While educators are cautioned from creating community norms in their learning spaces because of the ways in which these norms can take on the persona of the dominant culture, it is still beneficial to ask participants how they want the learning environment to be. Questions such as the following are worth exploring, because they not only create a better learning environment, but also provide participants with a laboratory to practice leadership:

- How will we hold each other accountable?
- How will we ensure this is a safe space?
- How can we make this space more inclusive?
- How will we name and resolve practices in this learning environment that are incongruent with what we are learning?

Physical space

The physical environment in which participants learn send implicit messages about the nature of learning that will take place within the space. When desks and chairs are fixed and aligned toward the front of the room, the arrangement subtly suggests to participants that the facilitator is the only person to be learned from and that their peers are not there to benefit their learning. Learning space structures where desks are grouped in a circle or quad structure suggest that everyone learns from everyone else. The facilitator for the learning experience might periodically shift the "front" of the room to further reinforce this idea. Tables may also be arranged in small workgroups to signal the idea that leadership is active and collaborative.

Learning Partnerships Model

Beyond shaping the culture and physical layout of a learning space, a pedagogical framework for teaching leadership can enhance student learning. Baxter Magolda's (2004) longitudinal study of young adults' development over their lifespan resulted in the creation of the Learning Partnerships Model (LPM), which provides a useful pedagogical framework for navigating varied developmental readiness for leadership educators. The LPM is guided by three assumptions (knowledge is complex and socially constructed; self is central to knowledge construction; and authority and expertise are shared in the mutual construction of knowledge) and three principles (validate participants as knowers; situate learning in participants' experiences; and mutually construct knowledge with participants) to promote participants' learning and development. These three assumptions challenge participants, while the three principles speak directly to the support that educators can provide. Table 1.1 contains some ways leadership educators can enact these principles in their learning spaces. Those who resonate with these suggestions would be well served to revisit Baxter Magolda's original work on the LPM and may find value in implementing these principles in their teaching and facilitating.

The Three Principles of the Learning Partnerships Model (LPM) for Leadership Educators

Principle 1: Validate participants as knowers

- Ensure participants' voices are valued through statements in the syllabus, the learning environment structure, and norms for participation
- Lessen the voice of facilitator as the sole authority by sharing expertise and experiences among learners
- Encourage active sharing of diverse ideas and viewpoints among all participants
- Help participants to view the facilitator as someone with experience, but still learning alongside participants

Principle 2: Situate learning in participants' experiences

- Encourage participants to share experiences and stories; combine with course assignments
- Implement the use of reflective journaling or online discourse via social media in curriculum design
- Be inclusive—avoid gendered language, do not rely on similar examples with which some participants are unfamiliar, include diverse authors and guest speakers
- Ask participants how well theories or models fit into their experiences
- Help participants see the applicability of content to their lives

Principle 3: Mutually construct knowledge with participants

- Position the facilitator as someone learning alongside participants
- Provide an explicit teaching pedagogy for participants in print or online
- Offer opportunities for participants to critique and refine existing theories or models

> Strategies for Teaching Socially Responsible Leadership

While the LPM offers some useful context for promoting learning and development broadly, there are several empirical strategies for fostering growth in socially responsible leadership specifically. One of the biggest predictors of socially responsible leadership is the extent to which participants engage in *socio-cultural conversations*, which are conversations about and across cultural differences (Dugan & Komives, 2011; Dugan, Kodama, Correia, & Associates 2013). Socio-cultural conversations likely have such large effect because they force participants to clarify and explain their own perspectives, seek other perspectives, comprehend how their values fit into a larger societal and political context, and discern how to work with different communities to create social change (Dugan et al., 2013) These socio-cultural conversations encourage *social perspective-taking*, which can be thought of as the ability to accurately infer another's point of view and/or empathize with their viewpoint. When participants discuss their perspectives and listen to others' perspectives, they are more likely to incorporate them regularly when they engage in leadership. Leadership educators would be well served to incorporate rich discussions about and across differences into their pedagogy, which may take on several forms including story sharing, case studies, and guest speakers.

Story sharing

Perceptions of leadership begin early in life. Participants might remember the teacher choosing line leaders for recess in elementary school or prominent elected leaders making a famous speech on television. The ways in which participants experience and understand leadership throughout their lifetime serves as the foundation for their current conceptualizations of leadership. Educators could find ways to have participants share their early, foundational memories of leadership and process potential differences based on the diversity of their experiences. Story sharing could also be used to explore why students want to study leadership and what their purposes are in life.

Case studies

Case studies can be invaluable pedagogical tools to promote social perspective-taking. With fictional or real-life scenarios prepared by the facilitator ahead of time, participants can explore how they would act in different situations. Facilitators may choose to assign participants various roles within the case study or let them choose based on their interests.

Guest speakers

Guest speakers allow for the exchange of diverse ideas in the learning space. Rather than simply inviting guest speakers who have particular expertise on a topic, educators might explore guest speakers who offer differing or contrasting views. Technology also allows for diverse speakers to engage with participants even if limitations in physical proximity exist. Video conferencing tools make it easy to host guest speakers from around the world. Social media also allows for guest speakers to engage with participants before, during, and after a designated amount of time when the group meets physically. Speakers more proximal to the classes experience (for example, seniors talking to sophomores) often bring a more approachable message.

> Active Learning and Leadership Self-Efficacy

Leadership is inherently active; so, too, should the learning about it be active. The chapters in this guide are filled with myriad activities and learning modules. The scholarship of teaching and learning, and perhaps our own anecdotal experience as educators, show that when active learning techniques are utilized, student learning increases. A meta-analysis of 225 studies of active learning across academic disciplines concluded that active learning increases student learning more so than traditional techniques such as lectures (Freeman et al., 2014).

The hope is that as learning increases, so too will *leadership self-efficacy*, which can be thought of as one's internal belief that they will be successful when engaging in leadership (Dugan et al., 2013). Research suggests two key experiences are especially beneficial for building leadership self-efficacy for participants: socio-cultural issues discussions (explored earlier) and positional leadership roles where participants have formal, designated opportunities to practice leadership. Although most learning spaces do not offer positional roles per se, the premise of providing participants with formalized opportunities to practice leadership is still a possibility. Many of the learning activities contained in this guide provide opportunities to build leadership self-efficacy for participants. When structured appropriately and coupled with active learning techniques, the possibilities for enhancing participants' leadership self-efficacy are strong.

› Navigating Resistance

Educators must recognize that while participants' understandings of leadership evolve, the process is rarely linear and without struggle. Challenging participants' thinking about leadership will often incur resistance, which can take the form of boredom, disruptive behavior, angst, or frustration. Some strategies for navigating resistance, widely informed by intergroup dialogue researchers (Maxwell, Nagda, & Thompson, 2011), are listed below:

- Recognize that resistance means you are pushing against something meaningful and significant to the student
- Avoid "attacking" the resistor—it will likely just cause more resistance
- Make sure you fully understand the source of the resistance by asking clarifying questions
- Explain pedagogical choices clearly
- Ask others for their thoughts on the issue being presented
- Gain comfort in dealing with resistance by letting it happen and working through it

Educators should probe why participants are displaying resistance by reflecting on their role as facilitators. Is the content too easy or difficult? Are there specific actions the facilitator is taking to cause the resistance? Ultimately, there is not a formula for working through resistance, but the greater the extent to which educators anticipate, recognize, and develop strategies for working through it, the more likely it will result in a positive learning experience.

> So How Am I Doing?

In a world where people are constantly bombarded with solicitations to evaluate the quality of service, it is often curious why educators do not ask for feedback more often from their participants. When facilitators wait until formal evaluations at the end of the learning experience to get feedback on their teaching, they are left with no opportunity to alter their practices to improve student learning. Here are some simple, yet effective ways to garner feedback:

- After a few sessions, ask participants to write down one thing they want to keep doing and one thing they want to stop doing on a notecard and turn it in as they leave
- Ask a colleague to facilitate a discussion with the participants to discuss as a group what could be improved
- Create a short online survey asking critical questions about your facilitation
- Schedule a consultation with the teaching and learning support unit on your campus

> Parting Advice

The goal of this chapter was to offer leadership educators some considerations toward meeting leadership education objectives and ultimately improving student learning. Teaching leadership is not unlike practicing leadership—to be successful, one needs to be thoughtful, intentional, reflective, and open to feedback. This chapter will be most useful if it pushes leadership educators to do these things as they engage in teaching leadership.

› Supplemental Readings

Angelo, T. A. & Cross, K. P. (1993). *Classroom assessment techniques: A handbook for college teachers* (2nd ed.). San Francisco, CA: Jossey-Bass.

Brookfield, S. D. (1995). *Becoming a critically reflective teacher.* San Francisco, CA: Jossey-Bass.

Brookfield, S. D. (2011). *Teaching for critical thinking: Tools and techniques to help students question their assumptions.* San Francisco, CA: Jossey-Bass.

Crosby, B. (2016). *Teaching leadership: An integrative approach.* New York, NY: Routledge.

Dugan, J. P., Barnes, A., Turman, N. & Torrez, M. A. (2017). *Leadership theory: Facilitator's guide.* San Francisco, CA: Jossey-Bass.

Owen, J. E. (Ed.). (2015). *New Directions for Student Leadership: No. 145. Innovative learning for leadership development.* San Francisco, CA: Jossey-Bass.

Seemiller, C. (2013). *The student leadership competencies guidebook: Designing intentional leadership learning and development.* San Francisco, CA: Jossey-Bass.

Snook, S., Nohria, N., & Khurana, R. (Eds.). (2012). *The handbook for teaching leadership: Knowing, doing, and being.* Thousand Oaks, CA: SAGE.

Svinicki, M., & McKeachie, W. (2014). *McKeachie's teaching tips: Strategies, research, and theory for college and university teachers.* (14th ed.). Belmont, CA: Wadsworth, Cengage Learning.

› References

Baxter Magolda, M. B. (2004). Learning partnerships model: A framework for promoting self- authorship. In M. B. Baxter Magolda & P. M. King (Eds.), *Learning partnerships: Theory and models of practice to educate for self-authorship* (pp. 37–62). Sterling, VA: Stylus.

Dugan, J. P., Kodama, C., Correia, B., & Associates. (2013). *Multi-institutional study of leadership insight report: Leadership program delivery.* College Park, MD: National Clearinghouse for Leadership Programs.

Dugan, J. P., & Komives, S. R. (2011). Influences on college students' capacity for socially responsible leadership. *Journal of College Student Development, 51,* 525–549. doi: 10.1353/csd.2010.0009

Freeman, S., Eddy, S. L., McDonough, M., Smith, M. K., Okoroafor, N., Jordt, H., & Wenderoth, M. P. (2014). Active learning increases student performance in science, engineering, and mathematics. *PNAS, 11,* 8410–8415. doi: 10.1073/pnas.1319030111

Komives, S. R., Lucas, N., & McMahon, T. R. (2013). *Exploring leadership: For college students who want to make a difference.* (3rd ed.). San Francisco, CA: Jossey-Bass.

Maxwell, K. E., Nagda, B. R., & Thompson, M. C. (2011). *Facilitating intergroup dialogues: Bridging differences, catalyzing change.* Sterling, VA: Stylus.

Vella, J. (2002). *Learning to listen, learning to teach: The power of dialogue in educating adults.* San Francisco, CA: Jossey-Bass.

Matthew R. Johnson is an Associate Professor of Educational Leadership at Central Michigan University and a partner with the Multi-Institutional Study of Leadership (MSL). His research focuses on the intersections of leadership, civic engagement, and social justice among college students. He completed his Ph.D. at the University of Maryland in college student personnel.

Chapter 3

Applying the Social Change Model of Leadership Development through the Use of Case Studies

José-Luis Riera & Matthew L. Creasy

> Overview

Leadership is a process that is learned from reflections on experience, from observation, and from applying new concepts like those presented in the Social Change Model (SCM) of Leadership Development. The case studies in this chapter are provided to illustrate the Social Change Model in action. Since leadership is expressed uniquely in different environments, these cases are set within the context in which college students and participants are probably most familiar: the college campus, and related environments such as an internship site or an alternative break experience. Leadership educators are encouraged to use these case studies with individual participants and groups as a tool to facilitate and apply their learning of the Social Change Model. The case studies in this chapter are designed to provide educators with a tool to use the SCM in action. At the end of each case study, there will be discussion questions that can be used to relate the case to each value of the SCM as well as the Social Change Model as a whole. This chapter is an update to an earlier version that appeared in *Leadership for a Better World* (Riera, 2009) and complements the material included in this guide.

Case Study Overview

Case study teaching can be an effective way to help participants experience the application of new concepts in a learning environment. What follows is a list of different ways case study teaching can be incorporated within the context of this facilitator's guidebook to suit the specific aims of a leadership course, program, workshop, or learning environment.

- Use the questions presented later in this chapter as a framework for analysis of the case studies
- Encourage participants to read the case study multiple times in advance of the discussion and application
- Challenge participants to take on one or multiple characters within the case study and react accordingly via role play scenarios
- Encourage participants to meet prior to a group discussion to act out and react to the case
- Have participants engage with the text rather than examine it by offering their own ideas of the process of the case, questioning one another, and debating the merits of various outcomes
- Remain active in order to draw students into the case by pointing out opposing views, asking participants to respond to one another, and asking the group to wrestle with its own questions
- Encourage the conclusion of case study discussions to be questions, not just articulated outcomes
- Help participants see themselves as a team of problem solvers and encourage them to approach the use of the case study in this way
- Use case study discussions as an opportunity for the group to set ground rules for its discussion—it is imperative that all ideas are considered and welcomed

Using a Case Study

Before beginning to explore each case study, consider how to use a case study most effectively. Case studies are not meant to lead to one correct answer, but to provide opportunities to apply new knowledge and practice analyzing issues from different perspectives. This is why it is helpful to examine case studies individually and with more diversity present in the group, the more perspectives may be present in the analysis of the case study. The following basic steps are useful when analyzing a case study:

1. Identify the characters in the case study—what is each of their roles?
2. Analyze the environment or context of the case study.
3. Apply the various C values and assumptions of the Social Change Model to illuminate the case study.
4. Design a plan to intervene or understand what is happening in the case study.
5. Compare the experience of the characters to personal experience.

A useful first step is to identify the characters in the case study. Who are the players? What is each player's role? The next area of analysis is often the context or environment of the case study. Although these case studies all take place on a college campus, there is a wide array of college and university environments, so it will be important to take note of the type of campus in which the particular case study is set. Then, identify the issues in the case study. What issues are affecting members' abilities to maintain positive working relationships? What issues are affecting the group's ability to reach their goal? What is the group's process of working together? How might the various C values be represented in the case study? Next, design a plan to intervene and propose potential solutions. Lastly, compare the case study to personal experience. How is it similar or different? How might the setting of the case study differ from the environment of one's own campus or environmental context? Is it realistic to imagine what is happening in the case study?

It is helpful to consider the benefits of using case-study analysis to understand how the Social Change Model might be implemented effectively. This type of analysis can provide challenges to conventional habits, promote the incorporation of multiple perspectives, assist in understanding the issue within a wide range of environments, consider the constraints that may be placed on the change makers by institutional or political forces (Stage & Dannells, 2000), and promote personal reflection.

The first set of general questions may be the most important. Their aim is to challenge one's instinctual reactions or thoughts about a solution for a given problem:

- *What is my first impulse on this issue?*
- *What the positive implications of that first impulse?*
- *What are the negative implications of that first impulse?*
- *How might the Social Change Model apply to this situation?*
- *How might knowledge of the Social Change Model modify that first impulse?*

(Stage & Dannells, 2000, p. 9)

The next set of questions fosters the consideration of multiple perspectives. Each person involved in the case will be affected by the situation in different ways:

- Who are the characters in the case?
- What roles do these characters play?
- What is the view of each character on the issues?
- What is the relationship between the characters of the case study?
- Which of the characters are also decision makers?
- What would be each of their decisions?
- Would some "invisible" characters be affected by the decision?
- What would be their perspectives?
- Who are other stakeholders or collaborators that might also be affected by the decision?

Considering the environment where the case study takes place is also an important element. These questions will help shed light on how the unique environment of the case affects the issues being raised:

- What is the history of the institution or place being considered in the case study?
- What is the relationship of the characters with the environment around them?
- How can you find good sources of information about the environment?

Finally, it is important to consider how the institution's governance puts constraints around potential solutions or provides supports for those solutions:

- What is the mission of the institution or place in question?
- Are there particular aspects of governance that need to be considered?
- What is the history of the institution with this issue?
- Do any political figures have any particular interest in this issue?

Particularly when one examines issues of social change, social justice, and inequality, it is important to analyze case studies with a critical eye. Analysis should include consideration of what is missing from the case as well as what is presented. For example:

- Are there individuals affected by the issue who have not been represented in the case study?
- Why were they excluded?
- How do characters present themselves in the case study?
- Is this so because of who they are?

Working with case studies can be a very insightful tool to help fully grasp concepts from the Social Change Model. Working within the parameters of a case study provides a safe place to try on different identities and consider alternatives in response to the presented issues for learning how one might respond in a real-world scenario.

› Applying the Social Change Model within the Context of a Case Study

The creators of the Social Change Model clearly intended it to be applied by individuals or groups. As a collaborative model of leadership, it encourages participants to get involved in group efforts regardless of whether or not they hold formal positions of leadership. While initiating change is important, it is also necessary to sustain the group's efforts over time. This means it will often need to be passed on from those who initiate the change to those who plan on keeping that change alive. In the college or university context this is best understood by thinking about how one's time on campus is finite. So, if an individual or group initiates change, eventually they will leave and depend on future generations of students to sustain this change (HERI, 1996). For example, think of a student organization with an ongoing tutoring program at a nearby elementary school and how they perpetuate a sustained relationship. We encourage you to think of approaches to these cases that produce sustained, systemic change.

The Ensemble highlights seven elements that are important to consider when planning any project whose aim is to affect social change. In no particular order, they include:

- *physical setting*
- *preliminary task definition*
- *involvement/recruitment of student participants*
- *task research/redefinition*
- *division of labor*
- *mode of group functioning*
- *legitimizing the project*

(HERI, 1996)

These seven planning elements are particularly relevant when considering how a change can be sustained—what elements need to be present in order to ensure that the change will continue?

These elements can be very helpful when thinking through the case studies presented throughout this text. The elements can serve as a framework to analyze and understand the case studies. With each element, think through how a change project that you are attempting to either initiate or sustain can best thrive.

The Seven Elements of Change: Project Planning for Social Change

Physical Setting Is the change effort at a college or university campus, the greater community, or a workplace? Within those areas, where exactly will the change be best initiated and/or sustained?

Preliminary Task Definition What is the need/problem? How do you know this is a need/problem? What changes are needed? How can participants best serve/solve the problem? What needs to get done?

Involvement/Recruitment of Participants What personal and shared values can be identified? Do the participants involved in the change process include those with diverse talents and backgrounds?

Task Research/Redefinition What additional information is needed about the problem or task and how might this information reshape the task?

Division of Labor How can tasks be divided most wisely among the talent that is held by the individuals in the group? What resources exist within the group of those initiating or sustaining the change?

Mode of Group Functioning What is the role of each individual group member? How can the group best collaborate? How can the group foster an environment where openness and honesty are valued? What knowledge and skill development does the group need? How will the group assess its progress and improve its processes through feedback?

Legitimizing the Project Is the community for which the social change is intended included in the change efforts? Who is the project intended to benefit? What are their perspectives on this issue? On the project? How can they be actively involved? Has the impact of this change been evaluated?

› Introduction to Case Studies

Three case studies will be presented in this text. The first is entitled "Who Knew Service had Challenges?"; the second, "The Intern's Perspective"; and the third, "Now What?" They will serve as an opportunity to apply the topics from each value of the SCM as well as the overall model and leadership in general.

> Case Study One: Who Knew Service Had Challenges?

You are a student at a mid-sized public university and are starting your second year of college. You participated in an alternative spring break service trip during your freshman year. For you, the experience was nothing short of amazing. You had never personally traveled to "The South," nor had you ever helped build a house for a family in need. You felt invigorated through giving back and creating something that will impact a life while countless others from your university spent time working on their tans. Each day had its high point and low point, and you always looked forward to evening reflections which helped you to process and create powerful bonds of friendships among your team. After the trip you waited with anticipation for the application to lead next year's trip, applied, and were selected to become a trip leader. You are ecstatic about this opportunity, and hope that your hard work and passion for the experience you had will pay off with a fantastic experience for the students on next year's trip. You, and your fellow leader, Melissa, will share responsibilities during the trip, and your staff advisor, Mark, will attend, as well to be a mentor and resource. The three of you have one training at the end of the semester, before leaving for the summer.

As summer comes to a close, you remember all the research you should have been doing over the past few months. Part of your role is to research the community the service trip will be engaging with, so that as a trip leader you'll be knowledgeable about the social justice concerns facing the citizens there. You send a text to Melissa but don't hear anything back, so you quickly spend a few hours researching the economics of this small southern town, the costs of living, how much rent is for a small family, and local crime reports. You discover how multifaceted affordable housing is in this town, and begin to wonder if it is like this all over the country. Surely if a sleepy town faces these issues, other major places must have them too? You place this information and some of your questions in a file to discuss at your first meeting with Melissa and Mark.

Being back in classes is more of an adjustment than you thought, even though the first week is mainly going over all your course syllabi. You and Melissa get coffee to talk about the trip, training, and the upcoming year. Melissa confesses that she really just wanted to go back for a second year to visit the town again, and you can tell she does not have a focus on creating the best environment for the trip participants, but rather for herself. You're surprised by this because during a group interview for the position Melissa spoke beautifully about her values of giving back to the community and creating an experience for her peers like the one she had. Furthermore, she also has not done any of the research she should have on the underlying issues facing the town, so you share with her what you have found and the questions you had about it.

Your first meeting with Mark and Melissa starts well, as the three of you catch up on summer work, vacations, and the new class of first-year students in the program. Mark discusses timelines for the trip and reviews expectations again. He asks what research you and Melissa were able to do over the summer. Melissa speaks up and shares the research you did, but never gives credit to you. She even poses your question about affordable housing nationwide as her own. You add in a few details that Melissa left out so you can contribute, but you don't mention how the research was actually yours. Mark seems impressed with both of you, and together you agree on next tasks.

As the semester moves forward, Mark has been training you and Melissa on what it means to be a successful trip leader and helping you to develop the skills required. You practice facilitation, how to read group dynamics, how to write lesson plans for reflection, and logistics information. You've held information sessions, received applications, conducted interviews and selected your team jointly with Melissa and Mark. By the end of the fall, Mark holds a wrap-up meeting with both of you. He expresses appreciation for both of your efforts and lets you know how proud he is of how far you've come. Whereas in the start of the fall semester Mark set out a timeline for you for work tasks, this time he allows you and Melissa to set the timeline, benchmarks, and due dates, with one exception. You need to get the timeline to him by the second week of January.

Personally, despite Mark being proud of both you and Melissa, you have misgivings about Melissa's work. She has repeatedly taken credit when she didn't complete tasks on time or not at all, and you've had to pick up the slack by doing the work for both of you. Melissa is better at facilitating and speaking in front of groups than you are, but that's only a part of the job to be done. You start to feel that Melissa truly is only in it so she can visit the town again as she stated a few months ago.

The spring semester starts with you having completed the timeline and sent it to Mark, not having heard from Melissa. Mark approves of the timeline and you start putting it into motion. You arrange to have coffee again with Melissa at a local shop. As the two of you catch up on winter break, the conversation becomes tense:

You: "Melissa, I feel like you are never up to date on your work and I'm carrying more of the workload than I should."

Melissa: "Well, I'm so busy with my sorority, I'm studying biomedical engineering, and I work two part-time jobs to stay in school. This is like the only thing you've got going on, so you can take on a little more from me to help out, right?"

You: "I understand that, but we both signed the same agreement to balance the work and work as a team. I'm not opposed to helping out if I can, but it isn't fair just to expect me to do everything without communicating." [Melissa grows exasperated.]

Melissa: "I hardly think you're doing everything; you barely speak in front of the group, and I lead every team meeting and work through your confusing meeting plans."

The discussion continues for a few more minutes before Melissa leaves. Both of you agree to touch base daily on work tasks and communicate if you are going to miss a deadline. You also will personally ask Mark to lead a vision and mission exercise to help both of you adhere to the goals of the experience.

The visioning exercise goes well and helps to develop an overall mission for the team of participants to view as their own. You also notice a change in Melissa; with group goals and values she seems more participative in the work, and your communications are more friendly than transactional. Rather than feeling stressed, you regain a sense of excitement about the trip. Before you realize it, the vans are packed and you are on the road. Having planned out reflections with Melissa was a great experience, as she brings a very different perspective to both the process of reflecting and the prompting questions.

During one night's reflection, the group was discussing themes of community and community values. Participants Tammy, Lisa, and Chris were engaged in the following discussion:

Melissa: "What do you all think are some of the values in this community and how do you see them in action?"

Tammy: "I think it's clear that this community has some rough spots, low income, and higher crime, but the rest of the community is trying to rally around and help others out through programs like this one."

Chris: "But almost everyone we've met here didn't grow up here, they moved or retired here. Except the homeowner whose house we are helping to build, everyone here has been here six or fewer years. Can we really say that they represent the full community? Can we really say that they aren't pushing values on this community that might not otherwise have been present?"

Lisa: "I've never seen a community like this one, where people truly care about their neighbors. Whether or not the people we've met were born here is irrelevant to if they are citizens here and acting for the community good. Would you reject positive change in your hometown because the people helping move it forward weren't born there? I think each new person can become an active member of a community like this, incorporate their values, and continue to move things forward. I think many of those we've met are more a part of the community than someone who was born here and simply lives here but doesn't contribute or give back."

Nightly reflections like the one previously described continue throughout the week. These discussions help the group to critically analyze their service, and ultimately bring the group closer together. As the trip comes to a close and you pack the vans to return to campus, you reflect over the eight-hour drive. How much has the service the group engaged in meant to the community? Helping to build one house surely can't transform an entire town—how can lasting positive change come from one brief week like this? You also consider the growth you've experienced in leading and creating change through this trip and the planning process.

> Case Study Two: The Intern's Perspective

Jake is a very confident first-year student. He arrived on campus already having connected with the university leadership program and is ready to show the world what he can do. Intending to double major in finance and economics, Jake dresses the part and regularly wears a blazer and dress shirt to floor meetings of his residence hall. Once the leadership program begins offering workshops for students, Jake attends as many as he can, taking up as much knowledge as he is capable of and making himself a regular in the leadership program office.

The leadership program office contains a lounge area that many students frequently hang out in between classes. Every fall the upper-class students eagerly await the arrival of the first-year students so they can get to know them and form new friendships and mentorships. Jake soon becomes one of the most regular faces at the table. The leadership program is run by two staff members, and Jake has developed a closer relationship with the junior staff member, Tom. Throughout the fall semester Jake and Tom debate and spar on a range of topics, from politics to history, economics, and even climate change. Jake views Tom as someone he can look up to and trust. Eventually, Jake asks Tom if he can serve as a reference and write a letter of recommendation for an internship. Tom agrees, but only if Jake will have a one-on-one meeting with him to discuss the internship and what he wants to get out of it.

Jake arrives for his meeting with Tom, ready to talk about all the ways this internship will be great for him. It's a high-profile firm, one of the biggest in the country, and to even get a foot in the door as a first-year student will pay huge dividends in a few years.

Tom: "Jake, tell me, what do you think this internship will do for you?"

Jake: "I really expect that it will give me the ability to advance quickly during my college years. Having an internship as a first-year with a firm like this is unheard of, and once I'm able to get the offer I'll be leaps and bounds ahead of my peers."

Tom: "But, what do you hope to gain from the internship itself; how do you think it'll change you?"

Jake: "I think it'll give me the chance to prove that I have what it takes to be successful in a fast-paced corporate setting."

Tom: "How do you think it'll impact your leadership style? You are in this leadership program after all."

Jake: "Well, I'm hoping to learn from the internship supervisor how to run things, how to make tough decisions, and what it is actually like to work for a company like this."

Tom: "Jake, I'm hearing a lot about what this internship can do for you, but not a lot about what you'll take away from it in continued development. Tell me, how would you answer an interview question about how your values align with the values of the company?"

Jake: "I highly doubt that they'll ask a question like that. I've talked with a lot of upper-class students, alumni, and business owners, and they've never mentioned their corporate or personal values. My father owns a business, and I can see what his values are with it, but he doesn't talk about them either. I don't think that'll be a real question they ask."

Tom: "Jake, I've observed some of what your values-in-action might be here in the office and in our program workshops. I think it'd be a good idea for you to think about how you'd answer that question, and how you'd grow through the process of having an internship. I also encourage you to journal throughout your internship so that you can look back and see how far you've come by the end of it."

Ultimately, Jake landed the internship with the company, a testament to his abilities and drive as a first-year student. He also became involved in the campus investment club, quickly becoming a vice president who oversaw fellow students in the organization. Before long, Jake sought Tom out again for more advice.

Jake: "Tom, I've gotten some feedback I'm not sure what to do with. Look, I'm very successful, I had that great internship last year with one of the top four companies, I'm a vice president in the investment club and I oversee seven other students and a number of the club's investments, and my professors all say that I'm in the top of their classes. The problem is all seven of the students I work with in the club are quitting. My internship boss said I didn't work well with others. I try. I try to get them all to have the same passion for excellence that I do, to want to do the great work that I've been able to accomplish. I want to help mentor students who are younger than I am. What am I doing wrong?"
[Jake and Tom have a long, in-depth conversation that includes additional feedback for Jake, and a realization for him that the way in which he approaches situations won't work for everyone.]
Jake: "So, I guess the way I come off to others can be off-putting."
Tom: "Well, think about how you encourage people, tell me about it."
Jake: "Actually I usually give them a hard time, make jokes about them not being able to handle the stress, tell them how quickly I'd be able to get it done if it were me. I think it motivates them."
Tom: "Now, imagine that I'm saying that to you about your performance here with the club. How would that make you feel?"
Jake: "It would give me the drive to do better, to show that I can handle what the person above me does, and that I could one day do the job better than they can now."
Tom: "Ok, now, you're close with Julie, who is your student mentor in our leadership program, right?"
Jake: "Yeah."

Tom: "Think about how someone like Julie would react if I were to give her that same feedback about her performance. How do you think she'd respond?"

Jake: "But Julie isn't a finance and economics major; we're different types of people."

Tom: "Do you really think that every person in your major is the exact same as you? When you're in a work setting or in a setting where you're managing others, you have to realize that not everyone is going to be the same. And that's part of the challenge. You've got to figure out how to encourage different types of people differently. Some people may be more like you and take the jokes as an opportunity to do better. Others will be offended and want to walk away. That's a good way to lose talent."

[The conversation continues, and takes a turn in a different direction.]

Tom: "Jake, how did you feel at the end of your work days at your internship?"

Jake: "I felt good—the work day was over, I'd completed my tasks or got them farther than my boss expected me to, and I'd head home."

Tom: "Did you feel fulfilled?"

Jake: "I mean, I guess. I'm going into finance and economics so I can make a lot of money and find fulfillment in other areas of life."

Tom: "Did you make any meaningful connections or mentors while you were there?"

Jake: "No, not really. Like I said I'd rather have that in other areas of life."

The following spring of his second year, Jake participated in one of the leadership program's service trips over spring break. The opportunity to serve others in need and see a different side of life caused Jake to consider not only what he wanted to do with his life, but how he wanted to do it.

Jake: "Tom, I've really spent a lot of time thinking about how and what I want to do with my life. I know I still want to run a business, I'm gaining the skills and knowledge to do that well. But a lot of what our conversations over the past two years have shown me is that there is so much more than a bottom line on a spreadsheet. After my internship in my first year, I had an internship over this winter break at a small company. You know what I saw? I saw people who worked late, not because they'd get a big bonus, but because they wanted to help out a friend—their co-worker. I saw it happen many times during my four weeks there and I never saw it in the entire summer I worked for the big company. That's the kind of business I want to run, Tom. I want to have a business that makes money—after all, that's one of the main points and needs—but also brings value to the lives of my employees. I don't just want someone like who I was when I look back, someone who just wanted to be there for a little bit, get a paycheck, and then keep climbing. I want people who will do the very best because they care and they know that my company cares about them too. I think, without having talked directly about it, that's how my father runs his business—he cares about his people and they care about us too."

❯ Case Study Three: Now What?

Dylan and Morgan, both in their sophomore year, attend Delmarva University. There are many aspects of student and campus life that are part of their experience, but perhaps the area to which they have deepened their commitment the most has been involvement in the University's leadership program. As first-year students, Dylan and Morgan both participated in APEX, Delmarva's leadership-oriented, extended orientation opportunity prior to the start of the academic year. As their affinity for learning about leadership continued throughout their first-year they were both approached to apply and serve as APEX Mentors for their second year. They each applied and were excited to both be accepted.

Delmarva University is a beautiful campus. Students attend from the entire Del-Mar-Va region (Delaware, Maryland, Virginia) and beyond. Recently, Delmarva has launched specific campaigns to increase the University's population of underrepresented students. A host of programs serving multiethnic, LGBTQ+, first-generation, and low-income students have been developed. Like many campuses, Delmarva is experiencing unrest as many students, and particularly Black students, join the Black Lives Matter (BLM) movement and give voice to what that means within the campus setting.

A student organization in support of Second Amendment rights has sponsored an outspoken national figure to come to campus and speak about responsible gun ownership. As part of many nationally televised interviews the speaker has conducted, she has come out against the BLM movement, calling it "anti-law enforcement." Upset that their peers decided to bring such a speaker to campus, a diverse group of students organized by the Black Student Union at Delmarva planned a peaceful protest outside of the event. By all accounts, the protest was a success.

Later that evening, a student reported to campus police that noose-like objects hung from trees in the same area where dozens of students stood in solidarity, peacefully demonstrating to encourage others to think about how negative rhetoric about African Americans serves to disadvantage them. Delmarva University was stunned. Police promptly began an investigation and campus leadership quickly began messaging about its progress to the entire campus. The university president visited students at the Black Cultural Center, and many stories about the sometimes unwelcoming climate of Delmarva University were told. Soon after, the police determined the entire situation was an unfortunate accident, showing that the noose-like objects were the metallic structures left in the tree that once donned paper lanterns as part of Delmarva's annual alumni festivities. Even so, the damage had been done, and this episode exposed the deep vulnerability of underrepresented students on campus, and Black and African American students in particular.

Noting the deep wounds, the university president called a late afternoon rally on the campus' quad to allow students, faculty, and staff the opportunity to gather supportively and share the stories of struggle that many endured on Delmarva's campus. The rally had a strong showing and the university president opened the rally by imploring honesty and the collective spirit of the University to overcome, while issuing a call for progress. Students then began to speak, and there was an open call for students to take the microphone and share about their perspectives and lived experiences.

Student after student shared stories that were difficult to listen to—stories that personified the marginalization of underrepresented students on Delmarva's campus every day.

Afterwards, many administrators and faculty stayed around the mall to speak to students. Once the crowds dissipated, everyone went their separate ways. While wrapping up work in their office, Delmarva's Dean of Students overhears two students in the hallway talking to each other. She looks out of her office to find Dylan and Morgan, two White students crying and talking to one another. She invites them in to talk. The Dean becomes acquainted with Dylan and Morgan and learns a bit about their story, particularly their involvement in the leadership program at Delmarva and as APEX mentors. Dylan and Morgan go on to explain that they were deeply moved by the stories of their peers of color during the campus rally. They articulated that they could not believe that the very university they had come to call home and where they felt so safe also has students that feel the very opposite—excluded, marginalized, and at times degraded. It was clear to the Dean that Dylan and Morgan were influenced by their peers' stories and anecdotes on a deeply emotional level.

As the conversation evolved, Dylan and Morgan explained that they "want to do something to help, but just don't know how to help or what to do." They spent time together with the Dean discussing ways they could be helpful to their peers, ways they could be more inclusive, and ways they could appropriately serve to make Delmarva a more socially just university. Eventually, Dylan and Morgan parted ways with the Dean and committed to begin talking formally about follow-up plans. Over the course of the next few weeks, Dylan and Morgan set out to make a difference. They would meet biweekly to have lunch in the dining hall with the purpose of talking about how they could be committed social justice leaders. They decided that they did not want to just join more groups, organize protests, or implore campus leaders to bring about change. Instead, they wanted to address the root causes of the issues that the students at the rally discussed. They wanted to bring out meaningful and sustained change. They wanted to be creative, and perhaps invent or introduce an innovative social solution to the negative climate that plagued Delmarva's campus for many underrepresented students.

› Supplemental Readings

Anderson, D. L. (2016) *Organization development: The process of leading organizational change* (4th ed.). Thousand Oaks, CA: Sage.

Barnes, L. B., Christensen, C. R., & Hansen, A. J. (1994). *Teaching and the case method: Text, cases, and readings* (3rd ed.). Boston, MA: Harvard Business School Press.

Boehrer, J., & Linsky, M. (1990). Teaching with cases: Learning to question. In M.D. Svinicki (Ed.), *New Directions for Teaching and Learning: No. 42. The changing face of college teaching* (pp: 41–57). San Francisco, CA: Jossey-Bass.

Brookfield, S. D. (2011). *Teaching for critical thinking: Tools and techniques to help students question their assumptions.* San Francisco, CA: Jossey-Bass.

Higher Education Research Institute (HERI). (1996). *Collaborative leadership for social change: Guidebook (Version III).* Los Angeles, CA: UCLA Higher Education Research Institute. Contains case study vignettes and can be downloaded at www.heri.ucla.edu/PDFs/pubs/ASocialChangeModelofLeadershipDevelopment.pdf

Magolda, P., & Magolda, M. (2011). *Contested issues in student affairs: Diverse perspectives and respectful dialogue.* Sterling, VA: Stylus Publishing.

Marshall, S. M., & Hornak, A. M. (2008). *A day in the life of a college student leader: Case studies for undergraduate leaders.* Sterling, VA: Stylus Publishing.

Olorunnisola, A. A., Ramasubramanian, S., Russill, C., & Dumas, J. (2003). Case study effectiveness in a team-teaching and general-education environment. *The Journal of General Education 52,* 175–198. doi: 10.1353/jge.2004.0005

Rowe, W. G., & Guerrero, L. (2012). *Cases in leadership.* Thousand Oaks, CA: Sage.

Stage, F. K., & Dannells, M. (Eds.). (2000). *Linking theory to practice: Case studies for working with college students* (2nd ed.). Philadelphia, PA: Accelerated Development.

› Media

Association of American Colleges & Universities, STIRS Case Study Resources homepage: www.aacu.org/stirs/case-study-resources

Center for Creative Leadership, Europe, Middle East & Africa Case Studies: www.ccl.org/Leadership/capabilities/europe/testimonials/casestudies.aspx

Harvard University, John F. Kennedy School of Government, Case web program homepage: http://case.hks.harvard.edu

MIT, *Sloan School of Management*, Ethics and Leadership Case Studies: http://mitsloan.mit
.edu/LearningEdge/Leadership/Pages/default.aspx

University of California, Santa Barbara, Case Method Website: How to Teach with Cases:
www.soc.ucsb.edu/projects/casemethod/teaching.html.

University of Washington, Daniel J. Evans School of Public Affairs, The Electronic Hallway:
http://hallway.evans.washington.edu

> References

Higher Education Research Institute (HERI). (1996). *Collaborative leadership for social
change: Guidebook (Version III)*. Los Angeles, CA: UCLA Higher Education Research
Institute.

Riera, J-L. (2009). Applying the social change model: A case study approach. In S. R.
Komives, W. Wagner, & Associates (Eds.). *Leadership for a better world: Understanding the
social change model of leadership development* (pp. 79–100). San Francisco, CA: Jossey-Bass.

Stage, F. K., & Dannells, M. (Eds.). (2000). *Linking theory to practice: Case studies for
working with college students* (2nd ed.). Philadelphia, PA: Accelerated Development.

José-Luis Riera serves as the Dean of Students at the University of Delaware, where he works to facilitate
campus environments that enable students to be academically successful, socially engaged, and personally well. José holds degrees from Muhlenberg College (A.B.), Colorado State University (M.S.), and
the University of Maryland, College Park (Ph.D.), and was a contributing author to the first edition of
Leadership for a Better World.

Matthew Creasy is the Assistant Director for Student Leadership Development at the University of
Delaware. He trains students on leadership and community engagement with a special emphasis on Alternative Breaks programming and creating campus change. He received his B.A. from Christopher Newport
University, where he was heavily involved in the President's Leadership Program and received his M.A.Ed.
in Educational Leadership and Policy Studies from Virginia Tech.

Chapter 4

Overview of the Social Change Model of Leadership Development

Steven M. Mencarini

Summary of the Key Concepts

The Social Change Model (SCM) of Leadership Development was developed by an ensemble of leadership educators and published in 1996 by the Higher Education Research Institute (HERI). This model encourages college students to think about leadership as an inclusive process rather than as a position, and is designed to enrich the development of leadership qualities in all, not just those in formal leadership roles. Social responsibility and positive change for the betterment of others, the community, and society is at the core of the model.

The SCM describes an interaction between seven key values (the seven C values) that individuals, groups, and communities should strive for in order to create the final C value of Change. These three levels of development (Individual, Group, and Society/Community) frame the Social Change Model.

The Individual level values are:

- *Consciousness of Self*—self-awareness, as shaped in part by the influence of others

- *Congruence*—fostering trust through authenticity; acting in accordance to one's values
- *Commitment*—sense of responsibility as determined by passion and investment

The Group level values are:

- *Collaboration*—the intent to work together by sharing responsibility, authority, and accountability, and thus multiplying effort, while gaining multiple perspectives
- *Common Purpose*—sharing one vision, though individual connections to it may differ
- *Controversy with Civility*—embracing differing perspectives; purposeful conflict that ultimately promotes the group's development and ability to achieve positive social change for all

The Society or Community level value is:

- *Citizenship*—seeing oneself as part of a greater whole, engaged in community and aware of issues that affect the entire group; forming networks and coalitions to enhance community

The implied eighth and final C value, *Change*, gives meaning and purpose to the other seven C values. Also included in the model are the reciprocal interactions between the three levels of development. Influenced by relational leadership models, such as those illustrated by Burns (1978) and Rost (1991), the Social Change Model views leadership as a process between people rather than a quality held by a single person or because of a title. The intent of the leadership process is to benefit others while altering and improving the status quo (Skendall, 2017). Since its creation, it has been widely adopted by college and university leadership educators in helping to ground leadership development programs with a theoretical framework and data-backed research.

> Supportive Research Findings

The Social Change Model has been utilized to inform a number of research articles. The Socially Responsible Leadership Scale (SRLS) was generated by Tracy Tyree (1998) to help measure the SCM values and how college students participate in a process of socially responsible leadership and has been condensed over time to shorten the instrument and optimize measures of reliability and validity (Appel-Silbaugh, 2005; Dugan, Komives, & Associates, 2006). The SRLS instrument has been used in a variety of research articles on spirituality and leadership (Gehrke, 2008), the effects of a liberal arts education (Seifert et al., 2008), and Greek life and socially responsible leadership (Martin, Hevel, & Pascarella, 2012).

The Socially Responsible Leadership Scale has been included as part of the Multi-Institutional Study of Leadership (MSL), an international leadership assessment completed by hundreds of colleges and universities and their students ("About MSL," n.d.). The MSL has been conducted six times to date since initial administration in 2006 with over 300,000 students participating ("About MSL," n.d.). Findings from the MSL have led to many research articles and dissertations ranging from articles on campus recreation and socially responsible leadership (Nesbitt & Grant, 2015) to race, gender, and student leadership behaviors (Rosch, Collier, & Thompson, 2015) to high-impact practices within student leadership development (Dugan & Correia, 2014). A sample listing of MSL-related publications can be found at http://leadershipstudy.net/reports-publications.

> Activities Overview

The purpose of the activities in this chapter is to allow participants to explore the various Social Change Model values. Activity One, *Co-creating the Social Change Model*, asks participants to construct their own model for collaborative leadership to identify critical elements, many of which will correspond to values within the Social Change Model. Activity

Two, *Exploring the Social Change Model*, allows participants to define and understand the relationship of the SCM values to one another. Activity Three, *Exploring the Interactions of the SCM*, briefly examines the interconnectedness of individual, group, and society values. Activity Four, *SCM Competency Self-assessment*, explores individual behavior and sees how participants may or may not be enacting socially responsible leadership. Activity Five, *Using Film to Analyze SCM Values*, can be used as to introduce the SCM or to help crystallize the entire model after discussing each of the Cs. Activity Six, *Crafting a Social Change Project*, challenges participants to think about creating positive social change while exemplifying the seven C values.

Estimated Time
Activity One: *Co-creating the Social Change Model*, 30 to 60 minutes
Activity Two: *Exploring the Social Change Model*, 50 minutes
Activity Three: *Exploring the Interactions of the SCM*, 30 to 60 minutes
Activity Four: *SCM Competency Self-assessment*, 45 minutes
Activity Five: *Using Film to Analyze SCM Values*, 20 minutes
Activity Six: *Crafting a Social Change Project*, 50 minutes

> Learning Activities

Activity One: Co-creating the Social Change Model[1]

Time: 30 to 60 minutes

Learning Outcomes   Participants will

- Identify their personal views on elements of collaborative leadership.
- Construct a model of engaging with others in collaborative leadership for change.
- Develop a heightened ownership and understanding of the elements of the Social Change Model.

---

[1] Developed by Susan R. Komives

Materials
- Half a pad of 3x3 sticky notes per person
- Pens for each person
- Wall or other surface on which to stick notes
- Markers
- Pad of poster paper

Detailed Instructions   This activity is used to build elements of the Social Change Model from the experience and perspective of participants.

Provide each participant with half of a pad of 3x3 sticky notes and a pen that will write boldly. Give the following directions:

"Take 4 to 5 quiet minutes to address this question—'what would someone need to know about, be able to do, or believe to engage effectively with others in collaborative leadership for positive change?' Write as many words or phrases you can think of on separate sticky notes. Examples might be 'sense of humor' or 'listening skills.'"

Divide participants into groups of 5 to 6 people. Give each group a marker. Have group members go to a wall surface and all put their sticky notes on that surface. (If sticky notes do not adhere to wall surfaces, put up a piece of poster paper for each group around the room.) Instruct each group to cluster their notes into themes or categories and try to name their categories. (If you have more time, ask them to connect their categories and/or have groups walk around and examine other groups' models.)

Ask one person from each group to describe their categories and read 3 to 4 of the sticky note concepts from each category.

As each group reports back, use a blank blackboard surface or poster paper at the front of the room to record key words. As words and concepts are shared, write them into a section of the paper that will cluster the individual elements, group elements, society/community elements (in a visual like the SCM), and a center section for anything related to Change. Draw a circle around each of the three domains, label them (individual, group, community), and draw a circle around Change and label it.

Affirm their good thinking and reframe their work to show how they just built the Social Change Model.

Facilitator Notes   Affirm that they know what it means to bring themselves to working effectively with others toward change. This is an inclusive activity where participants' thoughts are considered by the whole group. It sets the tone of inclusion and mattering.

Note that the society/community circle may be thinly populated, so put what you can into that domain. The prompt does not lend itself directly to populate that section. Participants may also have a hard time with unpacking the concept of Change.

This activity helps frame the concepts within the model. Follow-up with other activities that define the concepts in more detail. This is also a good opportunity to show the model as one approach to leadership. If the group identifies categories that do not fall into the model, they may be aspects that could be missing from the SCM.

Activity Two: Exploring the Social Change Model (SCM)[2]

Time: 50 minutes

Learning Outcomes   Participants will

- Be able to define the Social Change Model values and three levels.
- Understand how the seven C values and Change relate to one another.

Materials
- Masking or painter's tape
- Printouts with the definition of each C value and discussion questions related to that C value
- Slips of paper indicating the levels in the Model

Detailed Instructions   Using masking or painter's tape, "draw" the Social Change Model diagram on the floor using three large circles to represent the three SCM levels, and six arrows to represent the interactions between

---

[2] Adapted from Lee, A. M. (2010). An overview of the social change model of leadership development. In W. Wagner, D. T. Ostick, & S. R. Komives, and Associates (Eds.). *Leadership for a better world: Instructor manual* (pp. 32–50). A publication of the National Clearinghouse for Leadership Programs. San Francisco, CA: Jossey-Bass.

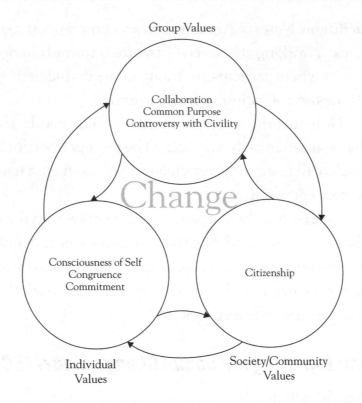

Figure 4.1   The Social Change Model of Leadership Development

the levels. Label each level with a slip of paper. At each circle, post the definition of the level, the definition of each C value in the level, and discussion questions for each C value (see below). The tape should look like the diagram shown in Figure 4.1.

Split the participants into eight groups and place one group at each value located in the circles. Ask each group to read their value definition out loud and discuss the questions posted at their circle. (*10 minutes*)

Ask the participants to move from one value to another value by either staying in their circle or following one of the arrows to another circle. Each participant can decide which direction they want to travel along the arrows when they leave their circle. Participants do not need to stay with their initial group.

Repeat the discussions at each value (eight conversations in total). (*30 minutes*)

When finished, ask participants to take a seat in the center of the model and share what they discussed at the circles, and to reflect on the concepts of social change and socially responsible leadership. If there is extra time, ask participants to offer their thoughts on the Social Change Model as a whole. (*10 minutes*)

Definitions and Questions for Each Value

Individual Values

Consciousness of Self

Consciousness of Self means knowledge of yourself, or simply self-awareness. It is awareness of the values, emotions, attitudes, and beliefs that motivate one to take action. People with a highly developed capacity for Consciousness of Self not only have a reasonably accurate self-concept but are also good observers of their own behavior and state of mind at any given time. Consciousness of Self is a fundamental value in the Social Change Model because it constitutes the necessary condition for realizing all the other values in the model.

Discussion Questions:
- Why is it important to pay attention to your Consciousness of Self?
- How can one improve their Consciousness of Self?
- Do you know yourself? Do you know yourself well?

Congruence

Congruence is thinking, feeling, and behaving with consistency, genuineness, authenticity, and honesty toward others. Congruent people are those whose actions are consistent with their most deeply held beliefs and convictions. Being clear about one's values, beliefs, strengths, and limitations, and who one is as an individual, is essential.

Discussion Questions:
- Why is Congruence important?
- Have you ever behaved in a group or a team with inconsistency? Why? What is the risk of behaving with inconsistency, with a lack of genuineness or authenticity?

Commitment

Commitment implies intensity and duration in relation to a person, idea, or activity. It requires a significant involvement and personal investment in the object of Commitment and in the intended outcomes. It is the energy that drives the collective effort. Commitment is essential to accomplishing change; it is the heart, the profound passion that drives one to action. Commitment originates from within. No one can force a person to commit to something, but organizations and colleagues can create and support an environment that resonates with each individual's heart and passions.

Discussion Questions:

- Why is Commitment important?
- Think about the commitment of the people in an organization you are involved with, or about the commitment in a relationship you are involved in. What can you do to improve this commitment?
- What can facilitators and participants do to improve their mutual commitment to the success of the class or workshop?

Group Values

Collaboration

Collaboration is a central value in the model that views leadership as a group process. It increases group effectiveness because it capitalizes on the multiple talents and perspectives of each group member, using the power of that diversity to generate creative solutions and actions. Collaboration underscores the model's relational focus. Collaboration is about human relationships, about achieving common goals by sharing responsibility, authority, and accountability. It is leadership for service.

Discussion Questions:

- Why is Collaboration important?
- What might be the negative impacts of a group not operating collaboratively?
- What does Collaboration look like in a group?

Common Purpose

A Common Purpose develops when people work with others within a shared set of aims and values. Shared aims facilitate group members' engagement in collective analysis of the issues and the task to be undertaken. Common Purpose is best achieved when all members of the group build and share in the vision and participate actively in articulating the purpose and goals of the group work.

Discussion Questions:

- Why is Common Purpose important?
- What might happen to a group whose members do not share a Common Purpose?
- How can you facilitate Common Purpose in a group?

Controversy with Civility

Controversy with Civility recognizes two fundamental realities of any group effort: first, that differences in viewpoint are inevitable and valuable; and, second, that such differences must be aired openly and with respect and courtesy. Disagreements are inherent in almost any social interaction or group process. They bring valuable perspectives and information to the collaborative group, but eventually they must be resolved. Such resolution is accomplished through open and honest dialogue backed by the group's commitment to understanding the sources of the disagreement and to working cooperatively toward common solutions.

Discussion Questions:

- What does Controversy with Civility look like?
- What may happen to a group whose members do not handle Controversy with Civility?
- Why is controversy important? Why shouldn't you try to avoid it completely?
- How might a group benefit from engaging in Controversy with Civility?

Society / Community Values

Citizenship

Citizenship names the process whereby the self is responsibly connected to the environment and the community, and where groups form coalitions to address community needs. It acknowledges the interdependence of all involved in the leadership effort. Citizenship thus recognizes that effective democracy requires individual responsibility as well as individual rights.

Citizenship, in the context of the Social Change Model, means more than membership; it implies active engagement of the individual and the leadership group in an effort to serve the community. It implies social or civic responsibility. It is, in short, the value of caring about others.

Discussion Questions:

- Can you explain the value of Citizenship using real-life examples? Why is it important?
- What are the communities you feel part of? How can you be active citizens of these communities?
- How might your primary groups/organizations join other groups/organizations to address community needs?

Change

Change

Change is the hub of the SCM. It is the center of the circles and the interaction of the other values of the SCM. Change, particularly Social Change, is the goal of the SCM overall. Change is not easy and can be uncomfortable, but is typically required to accomplish the goals of leadership.

Discussion Questions:

- Can you explain the value of Change using real-life examples?
- Why is Change important? Why is Social Change important?
- Is Change required to accomplish leadership goals? Why or why not?

Facilitator Notes   Encourage participants not to think that one level is better than another level. Everyone started at a different point in the model, but everyone also went through all three levels and all eight values. Though recent research supports the developmental sequencing of the Social Change Model from Individual through Group to Society/Community (Dugan et al., 2014), it is important to understand the seven C values, three levels, and Change. The interactions between and among each value and level are important to understanding the SCM as a whole. This activity can be done in combination with Activity Three: "Exploring the Interactions of the Social Change Model" to achieve this goal.

Activity Three: Exploring the Interactions of the Social Change Model

Time: 30 to 60 minutes

Learning Outcomes Participants will

- Understand the interactions between the Individual, Group, and Society/Community levels.
- Consider the effect of certain values on the effectiveness of the values/levels.

Materials
- Ball of yarn or string

Detailed Instructions Ask for three volunteers within the group and have them spread around the room. Announce that each of the three volunteers is a level of the Social Change Model (Individual, Group, or Society/Community) and the string or yarn represents the arrows between the levels.

Start the ball of string or yarn with the Individual-level volunteer. Have this volunteer toss the ball of string to the Group-level volunteer. Ask participants how the Individual-level values of the SCM can affect the Group-level values. After the discussion ends, have the Group-level volunteer toss the ball of string or yarn to the Society/Community-level volunteer. Ask how the Group-level values affect the Society/Community-level values. Continue around as the ball of string completes the first round of interactions, then reverses to complete the second round of interactions. Each time after the ball of string or yarn is tossed, lead a discussion about how the values interact related to the two levels connected by the ball.

Facilitator Notes This activity explores the arrows within the Social Change Model. Please note that recent research shows that there may be a sequential nature to the SCM values as capacity in the Individual level C values precedes capacity in the Group level C values which precedes capacity in the Social/Community level C value (Dugan et al, 2014). The concept of interacting arrows remains useful to illustrate the interactions in the model and provides a framework for formative assessment.

If the group is struggling to find connections, use the following prompts:

Individual/Group Connections: Consciousness of Self is a critical ingredient in forging a Common Purpose for the group as its members explore shared values and purposes. Similarly, the division of labor in Collaboration requires an understanding of each group member's special talents and limitations. In addition, Controversy with Civility often leads to innovative solutions and requires both Congruence (a willingness to share one's views with others) and Commitment (a willingness to stick to one's beliefs in the face of controversy). Feedback from any leadership development group is most likely to enhance the individual qualities of Consciousness of Self, Commitment, and Congruence when the group operates collaboratively with common purpose and accepts Controversy with Civility.

Group/Society/Community Connections: Responsible Citizenship and positive change are most likely to occur when the leadership group functions collaboratively with a Common Purpose and encourages civility in the expression of controversy. Conversely, the group will find it very difficult to be an effective change agent or to fulfill its Citizenship or community responsibilities if its members function competitively, if they cannot identify a Common Purpose, or if they pursue controversy with incivility.

Society/Community/Individual Connections: The community is most likely to respond positively to an individual's efforts to serve if these efforts are rooted in self-understanding, integrity, and genuine commitment. Responsible Citizenship, in other words, is based on self-knowledge, Congruence, and Commitment. An individual learns through service, and their Consciousness of Self is enhanced through the realization of what they are (and are not) capable of doing. Commitment is also enhanced when the individual comes to realize that positive change is most likely to occur when individual actions are rooted in a person's most deeply held values and beliefs.

Activity Four: SCM Competency Self-Assessment

Time: 45 minutes

Learning Outcomes   Participants will

- Become more aware of the SCM values.
- Gain knowledge about how they already enact SCM values.

Materials
- Copies of self-assessment (see worksheet at end of this chapter)

Detailed Instructions   After reading Chapter Two from *Leadership for a Better World* (Komives, Wagner, & Associates, 2017), think about how you either are currently demonstrating socially responsible leadership or how you have demonstrated leadership in the past. Complete the worksheet and identify how frequently you employ these competencies related to the values of the Social Change Model. (*20 minutes*)

Divide the participants into groups of two or three. Have participants discuss with their partners what actions they utilize to exemplify the various Social Change Model values. (*15 minutes*)

Invite group conversation after participants have a chance to discuss with partners to create a more robust exchange. (*10 minutes*)

Facilitator Notes   The Socially Responsible Leadership Scale (SRLS) is a tool available through the National Clearinghouse for Leadership Program that individuals and groups can use to assess their knowledge and confidence with each of the SCM values. This tool is available at www.nclp.umd.edu for a fee and may be used as a reliable and valid measure instead of the worksheet included in this book. Students who are using the *Leadership for a Better World* (2nd ed.) textbook may also be asked to complete each rubric at the end of the C value chapters and bring them as a basis for sharing and discussion.

Activity Five: Using Film to Analyze the Social Change Model Values

Time: 20 minutes

Learning Outcomes   Participants will

- Apply the Social Change Model values to a film.

Materials
- Film and equipment for viewing

Detailed Instructions   Have the participants watch a movie that encourages social change, such as *Selma, Amazing Grace, Milk, Made in Dagenham,* or *Remember the Titans.*

Discuss the movie and highlight the seven C values, three levels, interactions between the levels and values, and the ultimate goal of Social Change.

Facilitator Notes   Rather than waiting until the end of the movie to discuss various concepts, consider pausing the movie after key scenes that match well with SCM values or interactions to help frame participants' learning. If you are unable to screen the whole film for participants due to time constraints, participants may watch the movie ahead of time. Alternatively, you could only show key scenes and set them up with the story of the movie before showing the scene.

Activity Six: Crafting a Social Change Project

Time: 50 minutes

Learning Outcomes   Participants will

- Explore creating social change in a collaborative setting.
- Understand the basic assumptions of the Social Change Model.
- Relate their own groups' behaviors with Social Change Model values.

Materials

- Poster paper
- Writing utensils

Detailed Instructions   In this activity, participants will work together as a team to develop an idea for a social change project that affects positive social change. The point is not to implement these projects, but to explore the Social Change Model values as the projects are being developed.

Create groups of no more than five participants. Read the following scenario aloud:

You and your team members are a part of an organization and you have decided that as a group you would like to help address a need in the community. Utilizing the questions below, you will develop an idea to be executed by your team. You will have 30 minutes to work together to create your social change project ideas.

Distribute poster paper and markers for groups to write down their ideas. Questions for the groups to consider:

- Determine what is needed in your particular community. What issues or problems are prevalent in your community that you would like to attempt to address?
- What resources and assets already exist in your community into which you may be able to tap? What resources might you need to develop?
- What activities are you and your team interested in pursuing? What skills and abilities does your team have that you can leverage?

Work together with your team to list your potential social change project ideas. Now rank your ideas. Try to come to a consensus regarding your idea. If time allows, begin developing a plan to execute your social change project.

After about 30 minutes of groups working together, ask the participants and groups to wrap up their work. Rather than everyone sharing their ideas, lead a discussion on the Social Change Model premises and values. Have the participants journal first about the questions, then discuss as a small group, and report out to the larger group. Use questions like:

- Who demonstrated leadership within the activity? Was any one person "the leader" of the group? Potential topics to discuss may include the fluid nature of the leader-follower dynamic, helping participants see socially responsible leadership as a process rather than a position or role.
- Was the discussion and process inclusive? Why or why not?
- Which of the C values were utilized in the process of developing your social change ideas? Provide examples.
- Did your group consider stakeholders and community voices in your conversations? Why or why not?

Facilitator Notes   As the participants are discussing their social change projects, visit with each group to help them stay on task, answer any questions, challenge the brainstorming, and observe interactions where the C values are being displayed. It may add clarity to describe a community or context for all projects. If there is time, you could consider enacting these projects over the course of an extended period of time. You may also have the entire class focus on one social issue and each group work on a different aspect of addressing the root cause of the selected issue.[3]

❯ Supplemental Readings

Astin, H. S. (1996). Leadership for social change. *About Campus, 1*(3), 4–10. doi: 10.1002/abc.6190010302

Dugan, J. P., Turman, N. T., & Torrez, M. A. (2015). Beyond individual leader development: Cultivating collective capacities. In M. Evans, & K. Knight Abowitz (Eds.), *New Directions for Student Leadership, No. 148: Engagement and Leadership for Social and Political Change* (pp. 5–15). San Francisco, CA: Jossey-Bass. doi: 10.1002/yd.20149

---

[3] For an example of this type of activity, see the Social Change Project in Doerr, E. (2010, pp. 12–15) and "What is social change?" in W. Wagner, D.T. Ostick, S. R. Komives, & Associates (Eds.). *Leadership for a better world: Instructor manual* (pp. 10–31). A publication of the National Clearinghouse for Leadership Programs. San Francisco: CA: Jossey-Bass.

Higher Education Research Institute. (HERI) (1996). *A social change model of leadership development (Version III)*. Los Angeles, CA: University of California Los Angeles, Higher Education Research Institute. Available for download from www.heri.ucla.edu/PDFs/pubs/ASocialChangeModelofLeadershipDevelopment.pdf

Kezar, A. J., Carducci, R., & Contreras-McGavin, M. (2006). Rethinking the "L" word in higher education: The revolution in research on leadership. *ASHE Higher Education Report*, 31(6). San Francisco, CA: Jossey-Bass. doi: 10.1002/aehe.3106

Komives, S. R. (2016). 20 years of impact: The social change model of leadership development. *NASPA Leadership Exchange, 14*, 36, 38–39.

Reichard, R., & Thompson, S. (Eds.). (2016). *New Directions for Student Leadership: No. 149. Leader developmental readiness*. San Francisco, CA: Jossey-Bass.

› Media

Bruckheimer, J., Oman, C. (Producers), & Yakin, B. (Director). (2000). *Remember the Titans* [Motion Picture]. United States: Jerry Bruckheimer Films.

Cohen, B., Jinks, D. (Producers), & Van Sant, G. (Director). (2008). *Milk* [Motion Picture]. United States: Focus Features.

Colson, C., Gardner, D., Kleiner, J., Winfrey, O. (Producers), & DuVernay, A. (Director) (2015). *Selma* [Motion Picture]. United States: Paramount Pictures.

Heaton, P., Hunt, D., Malick, T., Wales, K. (Producers), & Apted, M. (Director). (2006). *Amazing Grace* [Motion Picture]. United Kingdom: Walden Media.

Karlsen, E., Woolley, S. (Producers), & Cole, N. (Director). (2010). *Made in Dagenham* [Motion Picture]. United Kingdom: BBC Films.

SRLS Online (website): thestamp.umd.edu/srls

› Professional Organizations

Association of Leadership Educators (ALE): www.leadershipeducators.org

International Leadership Association (ILA): http://ila-nct.org

National Clearinghouse for Leadership Programs (NCLP): http://nclp.umd.edu

Association for Talent Development (ATD)[4]: www.td.org

---

[4] Formerly the American Society for Training and Development

› Suggested Questions for Discussions or Assignments

- How have you become aware of the various approaches to leadership that you encounter daily?
- Can you think back to a situation where knowing the Social Change Model values would have been helpful in solving or discussing a problem? What were the circumstances? How might you attempt to resolve the issue differently?
- How do multiple perspectives and diversity fit into the Social Change Model?
- What is the role of ethics in this approach to leadership?
- How would this approach to leadership work in an organization with clearly-defined hierarchical positions of leadership? What benefits would it bring? What would be challenging to implement?
- How do you want your life to matter? What passions can you identify that are driving any of your actions, such as the major or future career field you are choosing?

› References

About MSL. (n.d.). Retrieved from http://leadershipstudy.net/about

Appel-Silbaugh, C. (2005). *SRLS revised: The revision of SRLS*. College Park, MD: National Clearinghouse for Leadership Programs.

Burns, J. M. (1978). *Leadership*. New York, NY: Harper & Row

Doerr, E. (2010). What is social change? In W. Wagner, D. T. Ostick, S. R. Komives, & Associates (Eds.), *Leadership for a better world: Instructor manual* (pp. 10–31). A publication of the National Clearinghouse for Leadership Programs. San Francisco, CA: Jossey-Bass.

Dugan, J. P., Bohle, C. W., Woelker, L. R., & Cooney, M. A. (2014). The role of social perspective-taking in developing students' leadership capacities. *Journal of Student Affairs Research and Practice, 51*, 1–15. doi: 10.1515/jsarp-2014-0001

Dugan, J. P., & Correia, B. (2014). *MSL insight report supplement: Leadership program delivery*. College Park, MD: National Clearinghouse for Leadership Programs.

Dugan, J. P., Komives, S. R., & Associates. (2006). *Multi-institutional study of leadership: A guidebook for participating campuses*. College Park, MD: National Clearinghouse for Leadership Programs.

Gehrke, S. (2008). Leadership through meaning-making: An empirical exploration of spirituality and leadership in college students. *Journal of College Student Development, 49*, 351–359. doi: 10.1353/csd.0.0014

Higher Education Research Institute (HERI). (1996). *A social change model of leadership development (Version III)*. Los Angeles, CA: University of California Los Angeles, Higher Education Research Institute.

Komives, S., Wagner, W., & Associates (2017). *Leadership for a better world: Understanding the social change model of leadership development* (2nd ed.). San Francisco, CA: Jossey-Bass.

Lee, A. M. (2010). An overview of the social change model of leadership development. In W. Wagner, D. T. Ostick, & S. R. Komives, & Associates (Eds.), *Leadership for a better world: Instructor manual.* (pp. 32–50). A publication of the National Clearinghouse for Leadership Programs. San Francisco, CA: Jossey-Bass.

Martin, G. L., Hevel, M. S., & Pascarella, E. T. (2012). Do fraternities and sororities enhance socially responsible leadership? *Journal of Student Affairs Research and Practice, 49,* 267–284. doi: http://dx.doi.org/10.1515/jsarp-2012-6245

Nesbitt, G. M., & Grant, A. (2015). Applying the multi-institutional study of leadership findings to collegiate recreation and athletics. In D. Stenta & C. McFadden (Eds.), *New Directions for Student Leadership: No. 147. Developing leadership through recreation and athletics* (pp. 19–31). San Francisco, CA: Jossey-Bass. doi: http://dx.doi.org/10.1002/yd.20140

Rosch, D. M., Collier, D., & Thompson, S. E. (2015). An exploration of students' motivation to lead: An analysis by race, gender, and student leadership behaviors. *Journal of College Student Development, 56,* 286–291. doi: http://dx.doi.org/10.1353/csd.2015.0031

Rost, J. C. (1991). *Leadership for the twenty-first century.* Westport, CT: Praeger.

Seifert, T. A., Goodman, K. M., Lindsay, N., Jorgensen, J. D., Wolniak, G. C., Pascarella, E. T., & Blaich, C. (2008). The effects of liberal arts experiences on liberal arts outcomes. *Research in Higher Education, 49,* 107–125. doi: 10.1007/s11162-007-9070-7

Skendall, K. C. (2017). An overview of the social change model of leadership development. In S. R. Komives, W. Wagner, & Associates, *Leadership for a better world: Understanding the social change model of leadership development* (2nd ed.; pp. 17–40). San Francisco, CA: Jossey-Bass.

Tyree, T. (1998). Designing an instrument to measure socially responsible leadership using the social change model of leadership development. *Dissertation Abstracts International, 59*(06), 1945. (AAT 9836493)

Steven Mencarini is Associate Dean of Students at Guilford College. Previously, he served as the Director of the Center for Leadership at Elon University for six years. He completed his Master's degree at the University of Maryland, College Park, and is currently working on his Doctoral degree in the Higher Education Administration program at the University of North Carolina at Greensboro.

Self-Assessment of Social Change Model Competencies

Using the scale below, rank your personal beliefs about yourself for each item:

1 = rarely, 2 = sometimes, 3 = often, 4 = frequently, 5 = always

Consciousness of self					
Ability to reflect	1	2	3	4	5
Meaning-making skills	1	2	3	4	5
Ability to give and receive feedback	1	2	3	4	5
Active listening skills	1	2	3	4	5
Congruence					
Action consistent with personal values	1	2	3	4	5
An ability to work toward a shared purpose in a group	1	2	3	4	5
Commitment					
Follow-through with commitments	1	2	3	4	5
Engagement and involvement	1	2	3	4	5
Devotion of time and energy	1	2	3	4	5
Willful action	1	2	3	4	5
Collaboration					
Strong listening, speaking, and reflective dialogue skills	1	2	3	4	5
Trust and trusting relationship	1	2	3	4	5
Shared ownership toward a Common Purpose	1	2	3	4	5
Common Purpose					
Ability to identify goals	1	2	3	4	5
Decision-making skills	1	2	3	4	5
Creative thinking	1	2	3	4	5
Ability to work with others	1	2	3	4	5
Ability to mediate and negotiate	1	2	3	4	5
Controversy with Civility					
Active listening skills	1	2	3	4	5
Communication skills	1	2	3	4	5
Engagement in dialogue	1	2	3	4	5
Ability to mediate and negotiate	1	2	3	4	5
Citizenship					
Ability to work with others across difference	1	2	3	4	5
Reflective thought/meaning making	1	2	3	4	5
Self-motivation/determination	1	2	3	4	5
Diplomacy	1	2	3	4	5
Empathy	1	2	3	4	5
Creativity	1	2	3	4	5
Critical thinking	1	2	3	4	5
Interpersonal communication	1	2	3	4	5
An ability to challenge assumptions	1	2	3	4	5
Advocacy	1	2	3	4	5

Chapter 5

∨

Consciousness of Self

Sherry L. Early & Matthew A. Cooney

◇

› Summary of the Key Concepts

Consciousness of Self is one of the Individual values of the Social Change Model (SCM) of Leadership Development. In order to understand how to effectively lead, communicate, and engage in relationship with others (Group values) or impact one's community (Society/Community values), it is essential to become self-aware and reflective. Consciousness of Self is an understanding of personal values, strengths, areas for improvement, and an awareness of how those beliefs and actions impact self and others. As unique individuals and leaders, you are constantly evolving with each new experience, relationship, and milestone. Therefore, becoming conscious of self does not occur in one moment or have a specified endpoint.

Important concepts related to Consciousness of Self include *self-efficacy*; *identifying core values*; *social-perspective-taking*; *empathy*; *mindfulness*; and *social identity exploration*. These concepts are directly tied to self-awareness, relationship building, giving and receiving feedback, and gauging one's self-efficacy.

Self-efficacy is confidence in one's abilities to accomplish a specific task; it affects participants' choices in activities and abilities to persist when challenges are presented to them (Bandura, 1977). Hannah, Avolio,

Luthans, and Harms (2008) argued that "leadership efficacy is a specific form of efficacy associated with the level of confidence in the knowledge, skills, and abilities associated with leading others" (p. 669).

Identifying core values guides how people live their lives, decide what is most important, when to take a stand, how they know who they are, and what they are not willing to do in order to reach a goal. "The exploration of leadership and culture is a journey both of discovery and practice, related to an understanding of self, an understanding of others, and an understanding of self in relationship and concert with others" (Ostick & Wall, 2014, p. 339). According to Selman (1980), becoming more conscious of self leads to becoming more aware of our world views, thoughts, and feelings; in turn, we become more aware of those same attributes in others.

Social perspective-taking involves challenging participants to view situations or consider someone else's point of view. It also encourages participants to become more empathetic. *Empathy* differs from Controversy with Civility because there does not need to be conflict. Rather, it is an appreciation for differing perspectives, considerations, and lived experiences.

Komives, Dugan, Owen, Slack, and Wagner (2011) defined *mindfulness* as the ability to "be aware of oneself in the moment, to be able to monitor and self-regulate one's thinking, behaviors, and emotional reactions" (p. 96). Being mindful allows participants to use their senses to focus and clearly understand a situation, and to be better-equipped to respond rationally and not emotionally. DeRue, Ashford, and Myers (2012) stated that mindfulness "is a 'state of being' where people are actively aware of themselves and their surroundings, open to new information, and willing and able to process their experience from multiple perspectives" (p. 149). Mindfulness differs from reflection in that it involves living in the moment and not making meaning of the past or planning for the future.

Social identity exploration consists of being aware of self and others with regard to dimensions of identity including gender, race, sexual orientation, socioeconomic background, religion, and more. Generational peers are important to take into account regarding culture, identity, and personal branding through social media (Seemiller & Grace, 2016). The Millennial Generation (born 1980–1995) are viewed as interconnected, whereas

Generation Z (born 1995–2010) has had access to technology and social media their entire lives and live in an exponentially more diverse world. Connected to social identity exploration are notions of power and privilege that exist at systemic levels and influence the intersections of identities and context.

› Supportive Research Findings

The Social Change Model has served as a guiding framework for leadership development programs for over 20 years. As the complexity of studies related to the Social Change Model increases, new findings have emerged related to how college students develop leadership. A significant finding about the Social Change Model shows the Individual level values of the model, including Consciousness of Self, serve as critical building blocks to develop group and societal values (Dugan, Bohle, Woelker, & Cooney, 2014; Dugan, Kodama, Correia, & Associates, 2013). It is important that participants consider Consciousness of Self early in the leadership development process as "understanding oneself in relation to others" and how it "augments the ability to foster social bonds and decreases in-group favoritism enhancing one's overall capacity to engage effectively in group process" (Dugan et al., 2014, p. 4). This developmental sequencing of the model does not mean that one learns each C value and is done, but does indicate that the learning of each C value is scaffolded, and the complexity of understanding each C value develops over time.

A significant finding related to leadership is self-efficacy, or the belief in one's ability to accomplish a task (Bandura, 1977). Leadership self-efficacy (LSE) is important because it leads to "increased motivation to enact leadership behaviors, gains in leadership capacity as well as performance, and the ability to reject negative external feedback including stereotype threat" (Dugan et al., 2013, p. 20). A deeper understanding of Consciousness of Self can provide a foundation for participants to reflect on their leadership self-efficacy.

LSE can be affected both positively and negatively based on societal images associated with what leaders look like and how they behave, especially for leaders from traditionally marginalized populations including different racial groups. Kodama and Dugan (2013) reported that sociocultural conversations with peers and positional leadership roles increased student leadership self-efficacy regardless of racial group identification; however, different leadership experiences predicted higher levels of LSE for different racial groups. These findings add to previous research on the importance of understanding the role of collective racial esteem (CRE) in leadership development as "positive impact of private CRE makes sense given that a better understanding of one's racial identity reflects a form of self-awareness" (Dugan, Kodama, & Gebhardt, 2012, p. 184). In essence, Consciousness of Self with respect to one's racial identities and efficacies in engaging in socio-cultural conversations with other diverse participants can positively affect leadership efficacy.

> Activities Overview

The activities presented in this chapter are designed to enhance participants' Consciousness of Self. In Activity One, *Identifying Your Core Value*, participants will explore their own values and consider how they relate to their leadership by exploring their most important value. In Activity Two, *Bag It!*, participants will work together to understand how perception and social perspective-taking are needed to engage in group work. This concept is actualized through a partner activity where one person describes a picture and the other partner draws it.

Activity Three, *Through Another's Eyes*, highlights the importance of empathy and oral communication to Consciousness of Self. The fourth activity, *Social Identity Exploration*, will allow participants to consider how their multiple identities impact how they lead, but also how others may view their leadership. This activity affords participants the opportunity to understand they possess many identities that are salient in their day-to-day activities. Finally, in Activity Five, *Mindfulness*, participants will engage in a mindfulness activity to illustrate the importance of being fully present when leading a group.

Estimated Time
Activity One: *Identifying Your Core Value*, 30 minutes
Activity Two: *Bag It!*, 15+ minutes, depending on group size
Activity Three: *Through Another's Eyes*, 20 minutes
Activity Four: *Social Identity Exploration*, 30 minutes
Activity Five: *Mindfulness*, 20 minutes

› Learning Activities

Activity One: Identifying Your Core Value[1]

Time: 30 minutes

Learning Outcomes   Participants will

- Be able to identify and share their core value.
- Understand how one's values lead to greater self-awareness.
- Consider how they bring their core value to life each day as a leader.
- Understand how a leader's core value can affect group dynamics.

Materials

- Paper (lighter colored, so you can see the values on the cards)
- Scissors to cut the value cards
- Binder clips for each value card packet

Detailed Instructions   Activity instructions, slides, and value cards can be downloaded at www.icarevalues.org/value_activity.htm

Distribute a value card packet (containing 40 value cards) to each participant. Ask participants NOT to look at the cards. Once the packets have been distributed, give the instructions that there are some cards with words and some cards that are blank; then ask participants to identify the values that resonate with them most.

Value packets include the following words:

Life	Compassion	Freedom
Dedication	Creativity	Accountability
Work	Religion	Humor
Cooperation	Trustworthiness	Advancement
Loyalty	Wealth	Security
Recognition	Beauty	Professionalism
Morality	Patience	Spirituality
Success	Responsibility	Power
Respect	Honesty	Empathy
Integrity	Justice	Health
Love	Faith	Helpfulness
Knowledge	Wisdom	Independence
4 blank cards		

---

[1] Activity adapted from Value Cards Activity. (n.d.). See: www.icarevalues.org/value_activity.htm

Give participants no more than 5 minutes to determine their Top 10 values from the stack of 40 cards. Remind them they can write additional values on the blank cards. Then, ask how it felt to only be able to choose 10 value cards. Now, have them remove 5 values and ask how they made the decision to halve their value list. Then, remove 2 more value cards and finally, ask them to identify only *ONE* value.

Facilitate a dialogue asking each person to share their core value while holding up their value card, and give a brief reason why. Ask them to reflect on how they arrived at this final value; what factors did they take into consideration to keep or discard the final 3 value cards?

(*Optional*: Ask participants to write a one-page reflection on what they learned about themselves by participating in this activity.)

Discussion Questions   The following discussion questions can be used to guide a debrief of the activity:

1. What were you thinking and/or feeling as you were asked to eliminate more and more values during the activity?
2. Which value was the most difficult for you to discard and why?
3. How did you determine which card you chose as your core value? Why is this value so important to you?
4. For those of you who chose to write your core value on a blank card, how did you arrive at this decision?
5. Does your core value connect to your leadership identity? Why or why not?
6. How does your core value influence your behaviors or actions as a leader? This final question can also be used as an optional reflective activity.

Facilitator Notes   Use the value cards without providing definitions to challenge participants more, and so participants can identify core values independently and justify how they defined the value cards. Add values that may be important to leadership in your context (for instance, faith-based institutions).

The value cards can be time-intensive to prepare (copying, cutting, and making a set for each person). Consider making a worksheet of the values if time is limited.

This is an activity for a group who has interacted at least twice before and may not suitable for group leader introductions. This can be a particularly powerful activity in a classroom setting or at a retreat.

Activity Two: Bag It![2]

Time: 15+ minutes, depending on group size

Learning Outcomes   Participants will

- Identify their strengths and gain an understanding of what others perceive their strengths to be.
- Assess and share ideas about the strengths of others.
- Engage in reflection based on the feedback of others.

Materials
- Blank paper (1 sheet per participant)
- Paper bags (1 per participant)
- Index cards (each participant should get one fewer than the number of total participants; if 10 participants are participating, then each participant should receive 9 index cards)
- Pens (1 per participant)

Detailed Instructions   This activity is appropriate for all group sizes; however, a minimum of 6 participants are recommended. Allow 15 minutes or more, depending on the number of participants. This activity is most appropriate for participants that already know and have worked with each other.

The room should be set up so that participants are arranged in a circle. Distribute a blank piece of paper and pen to each participant.

[2] Adapted from Majka, B. (2010). Consciousness of self. In W. Wagner, D. T. Ostick, S. R. Komives, & Associates (Eds.). *Leadership for a better world: Instructor manual.* (pp. 134–150). A publication of the National Clearinghouse for Leadership Programs. San Francisco, CA: Jossey-Bass.

Ask the participants to write a list of words or phrases that they believe describes their personality. Once completed, collect the papers and set them aside.

Distribute a paper bag to each participant. Ask the participants to write their name on the outside of the bag. While they are doing this, pass out the index cards (see materials list above to determine how many each participant should receive). Instruct the participants to open and place their bags standing in front of them.

The entire group should pass their bag to the person sitting to their right. Once each participant has someone else's bag, they should write 1 word or phrase on an index card that describes a strength, talent, or ability of the person whose bag they have, and then drop it into the other participant's bag. It is imperative to stress that the participants are only to write *positive* words about their peers. When finished, pass the bag to the right again and take the next person's bag and repeat. A suggested time limit is 1 minute per rotation. If some participants are finishing more quickly than others, a more structured and unified rotation schedule can be implemented.

All paper bags should rotate around the entire circle, until they arrive back to the original owner. Then have participants open their bag to find the index cards with words and phrases that others used to describe them.

Distribute the papers that contain each participant's list of words that describe themselves. Ask them to observe the similarities and differences between what they wrote and what their peers wrote. If participants would like, they can share their reactions. No participant should feel pressured to share.

Discussion Questions   The following discussion questions can be used to guide a debrief of the activity:

- What were some of the words that were similar on your lists? What words were different?
- Were there any surprises about what other people wrote?
- Do you think your own perceptions of your strengths are well understood by your peers in general?

- If you did this activity with "weaknesses," what differences might you see? Is it easier for us to identify strengths or weaknesses of ourselves and others?
- How much time do you spend thinking about your own strengths and weaknesses? Why?

Facilitator Notes   A writing activity can also be used to help the participants process the combination of all the strengths that others saw in them, and how they see themselves. Comparing the different words and phrases can help the participant identify commonalities about the 2 perceptions. This activity works best for intact groups or when participants have an existing relationship.

Activity Three: Through Another's Eyes

Time: 20 minutes

Learning Outcomes   Participants will

- Be able to identify that leaders see things differently based on their personal experiences and leadership identities.
- Understand others' points of views and perspectives.
- Consider effective oral communication techniques.
- Apply communication and social perspective-taking skills during the simulation.

Materials
- Paper
- Pens or markers
- Clipart or other stock images

Detailed Instructions   Pair up each participant with 1 other person. In each pair, have them designate 1 person as the sender and other as the receiver, and have them sit back to back. Provide the sender a picture of an image (keep it simple by using images like a ladybug, flower, house, etc.), which they will not show the receiver. Provide the receiver with paper and a marker or pen. The sender will need to orally communicate to the receiver how to draw the picture.

Tell the sharer they *cannot* share with their partner what the image is (for instance, "You are going to draw a ladybug"), and that they need to be descriptive by using shapes, size dimensions, and so forth. Allow the partners to communicate with one another in an effort to recreate the image on the blank sheet of paper.

Bring the group together and ask each pair to share the original and drawn images to the larger group. Then have a reflective dialogue on the challenges associated with the activity.

Discussion Questions   The following discussion questions can be used to guide a debrief of the activity:

- What was your reaction when you compared what was being described and what was drawn?
- What went well during the activity? What was challenging?
- Did the labels of "sender" and "receiver" force you into specific roles? In what ways did the "sender" receive information and the "receiver" send information?
- What did you learn about your communication and leadership/followership preferences?
- What did you learn about your partner's communication and leadership/followership preferences?
- If you were to complete this activity again in the same role, how might you approach it differently?

Facilitator Notes   This activity can be completed in several ways. Each pair can be given a very short amount of time to communicate their image, for example 1 minute, to emphasize the role of limited time in communication. Or, several rounds with the same partner could be conducted to improve communication or rotate partners to understand the importance of communication among different people.

Activity Four: Social Identity Exploration[3]

Time: 30 minutes

Learning Outcomes   Participants will

- Explore their various social identities.
- Understand how social identities affect an individual's thoughts on leadership.

Materials
- Social identity worksheet (see worksheet at end of this chapter)
- Pens or markers

Detailed Instructions   Begin the discussion by speaking about social identity and the various types of social identities (race, ethnicity, gender identity and expression, sex, sexual orientation, size, age, religion, ability, etc.) that exist. It is best if facilitators familiarize themselves with the social identity groups listed below, as well as developing an understanding of privilege, power, and difference. Goodman (2010) provides a brief introduction to social identity topic. Jones and Abes (2013) go into more depth on identity development, particularly related to the Model of Multiple Dimensions of Identity (MMDI).

Distribute the social identity worksheet (see the worksheet at end of chapter). Explain that this worksheet contains only some social identities, and encourage participants to write in social identities that may not be covered, yet still have significance. Ask participants to complete the social identity worksheet individually. Allow participants to ask questions

---

[3] Adapted from The Program on Intergroup Relations, National Intergroup Dialogue Institute. (2013). *Social Identity Profile-Community Impact Version*. University of Michigan. Retrieved August 04, 2016, from https://docs.google.com/file/d/0B7jitSX6H2o1bUxMNG5rX1B0SW9xODYxd2lZUWdVVEc0VWhB/edit. Used with permission.

about what a social identity may mean, but allow participants to decide for themselves how they may identify.

Ask participants to discuss in pairs for 5 to 10 minutes how they felt marking down their own identities.

Bring the discussion back to the larger group. Direct participants to consider how their social identities impact their leadership efficacy/capacity:

- What social identity impacts the way that you enact your leadership skills?
- What social identity do you feel does not affect your leadership skills?
- How do other people's social identities affect the way that you view their leadership skills?

Discussion Questions   The following discussion questions can be used to guide a debrief of the activity:

- How can you engage with others about how their identities may impact their work as a leader?
- Can you identify any famous leaders throughout history and how their work may be perceived differently if they held different identities?
- Why is it important that we acknowledge our own, as well as other groups' members and social identities within the context of leadership?
- What resources can you use in your organization to learn more about social identity and its impact on leadership?
- What will you take from this activity as you lead your group in both passive and active ways?

Facilitator Notes   This activity is designed for introducing participants to social identities. Depending on the developmental maturity of the group, conversation can include deeper processing about privilege, power, and oppression at the individual and systemic levels. You might also consider adapting the Model of Multiple Dimensions of Identity (Jones & Abes, 2013) to explore intersecting identities.

Activity Five: Mindfulness[4]

Time: 20 minutes

Learning outcomes   Participants will

- Learn a strategy to engage in mindfulness.
- Reflect on how mindfulness is related to Consciousness of Self.
- Discuss how mindfulness may impact leadership.

Materials
- 1 raisin per participant (another small dried fruit could also be used)
- Paper
- Pens or markers

Detailed Instructions   Begin by discussing leadership and the need for leaders to be fully present when engaging with other group members. Explain that the only behavior and thoughts that a leader can control in a group setting are the leader's own. One way to practice control of mind and thoughts is through mindfulness.

Pass out 1 raisin to each person. Additionally, pass out 1 sheet of paper and a pen or marker. Explain that the group will be participating in a mindfulness exercise and that it is best to minimize all distractions during the activity including talking and use of cell phones. Begin the activity by following the script below:

Holding: Close your eyes and hold the raisin in your hand. Rub it between your fingers. Pay attention to how it feels. Is it soft? Hard? Do you feel any grooves or crevices? Really focus on it. Does one side differ more than the other? (Give participants about 1 minute to complete holding the raisin.)
Seeing: Now look at the raisin. Look at all sides of it. Is there anything that you notice now that you didn't before? What is different about the raisin?

---

[4] Adapted from Williams, M., Teasdale, J., Segal, Z., & Kabat-Zinn, J. (2007). *The mindful way through depression: Freeing yourself from chronic unhappiness.* New York, NY: Guilford Press. Reprinted with permission of Guilford Press.

What makes this raisin different from other raisins that you have seen previously? Pretend that you need to describe the raisin to someone that has never seen one before. What would you say? (Give participants about 1 minute to complete seeing the raisin.)

Smelling: Smell the raisin. How would you describe it to others? Does it change with each inhalation? What is happening to your stomach when you inhale? (Give participants about 1 minute to complete smelling the raisin.)

Placing: Place the raisin in your mouth, but do not chew. Where is it sitting in your mouth? Can you feel where each part of the raisin lays in your mouth? Place it in different sides of your mouth and think about how it feels. Really focus on the location in your mouth. How did it get there? Is that the best place for it? (Give participants about 1 minute to feel the raisin in mouth.)

Tasting: Begin to chew the raisin. Slowly chew it. Consider what teeth you use to chew it. How many bites does it take? Is each bite different? The same? What happens to the raisin? Is in different places? How would you describe the taste to others? (Give participants about 1 minute to complete tasting the raisin.)

Swallowing: As you swallow the raisin, pay attention to where it goes within your body. Are you able to feel it move down your mouth?

Discussion Questions   The following discussion questions can be used to guide a debrief of the activity:

- How was this exercise for you?
- To what degree do you engage in mindfulness behaviors when working in groups?
- Can you connect mindfulness to your leadership behaviors?
- How do you engage in mindfulness when supporting other leaders?
- Can you describe a time when it would have been beneficial to engage in mindfulness when working in a group?

Facilitator Notes   Various video clips that have guided raisin mindfulness meditations are available online (for example, see "What a

Raisin Can Teach You about Mindfulness Practice" by Clare Josa at http://youtu.be/z2Eo56BLMjM). If there are participants who have visual, hearing, or other impairments, it is possible to modify this activity and still execute it effectively.

› Supplemental Readings

Bandura, A. (1997). *Self-efficacy: The exercise of control.* New York, NY: Freeman.

George, B. (2012, October 26). Mindfulness helps you become a better leader. *Harvard Business Review.* Retrieved from https://hbr.org/2012/10/mindfulness-helps-you-become-a

Osteen, L., Owen, J. E., Komives, S. R., Mainella, F. C., & Longerbeam, S. D. (2006). A leadership identity development model: Applications from a grounded theory. *Journal of College Student Development, 47*(x), 401–418. doi: 10.1353/csd.2006.0048

Reichard, R., & Thompson, S. (Eds.). (2016). *New Directions for Student Leadership: No. 149. Leader developmental readiness.* San Francisco, CA: Jossey-Bass.

› Media

Andy Puddicombe (2012). TED Talk: All it takes is 10 mindful minutes. Retrieved from: www.ted.com/talks/andy_puddicombe_all_it_takes_is_10_mindful_minutes

UCLA Mindful Awareness Research Center (Producer). (2009–2014). *Mindfulness Meditations* [audio podcasts]. Retrieved from: http://marc.ucla.edu/body.cfm?id=22

Mindfulness for Students (Producer). (2013). *Free audio guided practices* [audio podcasts]. Retrieved from: http:// http://mindfulnessforstudents.co.uk/resources/mindfulness-audio-guided-practices

Clare Josa (2012, February 12). *What a raisin can teach you about mindfulness* [Video file]. Retrieved from: http://youtu.be/z2Eo56BLMjM

What do you see? (n.d.) *Creducation.org.* Retrieved from: www.creducation.org/resources/perception_checking/What_Do_You_See_Activity_OCDRCM.pdf

Classroom Activities on perspective taking (n.d.). *Creducation.org.* Retrieved from: www.creducation.org/resources/perception_checking/classroom_activities_on_perspective_taking.html

Dr. Brené Brown (2013, December 10). Brené Brown on Empathy [Video file]. Retrieved from: http://youtube.com/watch?v=1Evwgu369Jw

Value cards activity (n.d.). *icarevalues.org*. Retrieved from: http://www.icarevalues.org/value_activity.htm

Social Identity Groups (n.d.). *The National Intergroup Dialogue Institute*. Retrieved from: millere.wiki.farmington.k12.mi.us/file/view/Social+Identity+Profile-Standard+Version.doc

› Professional Organizations

ACPA Commission for Student Involvement: www.myacpa.org/commsi

Association of Leadership Educators: www.leadershipeducators.org

International Leadership Association: www.ila-net.org

Leadership Education Academy: www.ila-net.org/lea/

Leadership Educator's Institute: www.myacpa.org/events/leadership-educators-institute

NASPA Knowledge Community for Student Leadership Programs: www.naspa.org/constituent-groups/kcs/student-leadership-programs

National Clearinghouse for Leadership Programs: http://nclp.umd.edu

National Collegiate Leadership Conference: http://leadership.arizona.edu/national-collegiate-leadership-conference

› Other Resources

Many survey-style instruments exist to help expand participants' self-awareness, particularly in areas of personal style. While many of these types of assessments are available online, it is often preferable to have a qualified professional review the results of the assessment in order to fully understand its meaning. The following are a few assessments that are often used in campus leadership development programs:

Socially Responsible Leadership Scale: http://nclp.umd.edu

Myers-Briggs Type Indicator: www.mbticomplete.com

True Colors: www.truecolors.org

The Leadership Practices Inventory: www.lpionline.com

Gallup StrengthsQuest: www.strengthsquest.com

DISC: discpersonalitytesting.com

16 Personalities: www.16personalities.com

Keirsey Temperament Sorter: www.keirsey.com

9types.com: www.9types.com.

The Big Five Personality Test: www.truity.com/test/big-five-personality-test

Johari Window: www.mindtools.com/CommSkll/JohariWindow.htm

> Suggested Questions for Discussions or Assignments

- How would having a conscious awareness of your values and beliefs influence your leadership? What are specific examples of this?
- How are leadership capacity and leadership self-efficacy connected? How are they distinct?
- How would the group values of Collaboration, Common Purpose, and Controversy with Civility work differently if everyone in the group were able to practice mindfulness?
- What strengths does your personal style bring to working in groups? In what ways does your style sometimes make group work challenging?
- What are the personal values that guide how you interact in groups? How do you approach citizenship in your communities? What values guide your approach to citizenship and civic engagement?
- What format of reflection (for example, journaling, quiet time for thought, a discussion partner or group) would be most realistic for you to take up as a regular practice of examining who you are? This week, try a format you have never used before. Does using a different format change the nature of your reflection?
- Do you seek feedback? How do you react when others give you feedback? Think of someone with whom you have engaged in leadership processes and ask them for feedback on your strengths and areas for growth.

> References

Bandura, A. (1977). Self-efficacy: Toward a unifying theory of behavioral change. *Psychological review 84*, 191–215. doi: 10.1037//0033-295X.84.2.191

DeRue, D. S., Ashford, S. J., & Myers, C. G. (2012). Learning agility: In search of conceptual clarity and theoretical grounding. *Industrial and Organizational Psychology, 5*, 258–279. doi:10.1111/j.1754-9434.2012.01444.x

Dugan, J. P., Bohle, C. W., Woelker, L. R., & Cooney, M. A. (2014). The role of social perspective-taking in developing students' leadership capacities. *Journal of Student Affairs Research and Practice*, *51*, 1–15. doi:10.1515/jsarp-2014-0001

Dugan, J. P., Kodama, C., Correia, B., & Associates. (2013). *Multi-institutional study of leadership insight report: Leadership program delivery.* College Park, MD: National Clearinghouse for Leadership Programs.

Goodman, D. J. (2010). Helping students explore their privileged identities. *Diversity and Democracy*, *13*(2), 10–12. Washington, DC: AAC&U. Retrieved from: www.aacu.org/publications-research/periodicals/helping-students-explore-their-privileged-identities

Hannah, S. T., Avolio, B. J., Luthans, F., & Harms, P. D. (2008). Leadership efficacy: Review and future directions. *The Leadership Quarterly*, *19*, 669–692. doi: 10.1016/j.leaqua.2008.09.007

Jones, S. R., & Abes, E. S. (2013). *Identity development in college students: Advancing the model of multiple dimensions of identity.* San Francisco, CA: Jossey-Bass.

Kodama, C. M., & Dugan, J. P. (2013). Leveraging leadership efficacy for college students: Disaggregating data to examine unique predictors by race. *Equity & Excellence in Education*, *46*, 184–201. doi: 10.1080/10665684.2013.780646

Komives, S. R., Dugan, J. P., Owen, J. E., Slack, C., & Wagner, W. (2011). *The handbook for student leadership development.* San Francisco, CA: Jossey-Bass.

Majka, B. (2010). Consciousness of self. In W. Wagner, D. T. Ostick, S. R. Komives, & Associates (Eds.), *Leadership for a better world: Instructor manual* (pp. 134–150). A publication of the National Clearinghouse for Leadership Programs. San Francisco, CA: Jossey-Bass.

Ostick, D. T., & Wall, V. A. (2011). Considerations for culture and social identity dimensions. In S. R. Komives, J. P. Dugan, J. E. Owen, W. Wagner, C. Slack, & Associates, *Handbook for student leadership development* (pp. 339–368). San Francisco, CA: Jossey-Bass.

The Program on Intergroup Relations, National Intergroup Dialogue Institute. (2013). Social Identity Profile-Community Impact Version. University of Michigan. Retrieved from: https://docs.google.com/file/d/0B7jitSX6H2o1bUxMNG5rX1B0 SW9xODYxd2lZUWdVVEc0VWhB/edit

Seemiller, C., & Grace, M. (2016). *Generation Z goes to college.* San Francisco, CA: Jossey-Bass.

Selman, R. L. (1980). *The growth of interpersonal understanding: Developmental and clinical analyses.* New York, NY: Academic Press.

Value cards activity (n.d.). *icarevalues.org*. Retrieved from: http://www.icarevalues.org/value_activity.htm

Williams, M., Teasdale, J., Segal, Z., & Kabat-Zinn, J. (2007). *The mindful way through depression: Freeing yourself from chronic unhappiness*. New York, NY: Guilford Press.

Sherry L. Early is an assistant professor in the Leadership Studies program at Marshall University. Her most recent publication is "An Examination of Mentoring Relationships and Leadership Capacity in Resident Assistants" in ACUHO i'o 2016 Special Topic Edition centered on resident assistants in the *Journal of College and University Student Housing*. She is co-author of the Consciousness of Self chapter in the 2nd edition of *Leadership for a Better World*.

Matthew A. Cooney is a doctoral candidate at Bowling Green State University. He received his master's degree from Loyola University Chicago where he served on the Multi-Institutional Study of Leadership research team.

Social Identity Worksheet

Social Identity	Group Membership	Most affects how you understand leadership	Least affects how you understand leadership	Most affects how OTHERS view your leadership	Least affects how OTHERS view your leadership
Gender Identity and Expression					
Sex					
Race					
Ethnicity					
Sexual Orientation					
Religion					
Social Class					
Age					
(Dis)Ability					
Nation(s) of Origin and/or Citizenship					
Body size					
Additional					

Adapted from The Program on Intergroup Relations, National Intergroup Dialogue Institute. (2013). Social Identity Profile-Community Impact Version. University of Michigan. Retrieved from: https://docs.google .com/file/d/0B7jitSX6H2o1bUxMNG5rX1B0SW9xODYxd2lZUWdVVEc0VWhB/edit. Used with permission.

Chapter 6

Congruence

Shamika N. Karikari

> Summary of the Key Concepts

Congruence, one of the Individual level values of the Social Change Model (SCM) of Leadership Development, is very closely connected to Consciousness of Self, as the work of being a person of Congruence begins with the work of understanding oneself. However, Congruence takes that self-awareness one step further. It asks that we align our interior beliefs and values with our exterior actions and behaviors. This means that our espoused values match our enacted values.

Congruence examines how you live your personal values. It is easy for people to identify their personal values; however, this chapter prompts readers to consider how their actions align with those stated values. This chapter provides learning activities for participants to examine their own personal values. After doing so, participants are encouraged to observe the nuances associated with Congruence in everyday life. Each activity allows participants to reflect on congruence and realize that congruence is not always black and white. Even with the best intentions, we do not always make decisions that align with our personal values.

> Supportive Research Findings

Research on the Congruence value highlights the connection to spirituality. Gehrke (2008) found that "the desire to form a meaningful philosophy of life, inherent in spiritual quest, relate to the value of Congruence" (p. 356). The relationship between spirituality and Congruence is distinct because of their interconnectedness. As Gehrke suggests, spirituality focuses on finding how you make meaning in your life and what you value. This directly connects to Congruence and how it focuses on your decisions connecting to what you value. Spirituality and Congruence are uniquely intertwined.

> Activities Overview

Activity One, *My Values*, is a reflection exercise that allows participants to reflect on their personal values as a foundation for learning about Congruence. The second activity, *Values in Movies*, asks participants to view movie clips and identify how values and congruent behavior play out in those scenarios. In Activity Three, *Sharing Stories*, participants share personal stories from their lives that demonstrate Congruence and incongruence. In the fourth activity, *Scenarios*, participants take their knowledge of Congruence and put it into action by examining unique situations and identifying how they would respond in those situations. In the final activity, *Contextualized Me*, participants will explore their identities and their interplay with the contexts in which they exist. Each of these activities builds sequentially on one another and it is suggested that they are led in order, or that the first activity precedes any of the others.

Estimated Time

Activity One: *My Values*, 5 to 10 minute activity, 10 to 20 minute reflective discussion

Activity Two: *Values in Movies*, 15 minutes of movie clips, 15 to 30 minute reflective discussion

Activity Three: *Sharing Stories*, 20 to 30 minutes in pairs or groups of 3, 15 to 20 minute large group discussion

Activity Four: *Scenarios*, 15 minute small group discussion, 15 to 30 minute large group discussion

Activity Five: *Contextualized Me*, 30 to 60 minutes

› Learning Activities

Activity One: My Values

Time: 15 to 30 minutes

Learning Outcomes   Participants will

- Be able to identify the personal values that are most important to them.
- Understand how their personal values influence their leadership approach.

Materials
- Writing utensils
- Paper
- Board or screen (if not using worksheet)
- Worksheet with questions (if not using board or screen)

Detailed Instructions   Create a worksheet with the questions listed below, or have the questions on a screen or board for all participants to see. Have participants answer the following questions silently (*5 to 10 minutes*):

- What five personal values are the most important to you? How are each of these values important?
- What value do you consider most as a leader?
- How do your values influence your leadership style? Give specific examples.

- How often do you consciously think about your values?
- How do your values align or not with this group? (This group could also be replaced with a specific organization, team, or other affinity group.)
- What do you do when your values come into conflict?

After participants have completed these questions, have them break into small groups of 3 to 5 people and share their values and other highlights from their reflections. (*10 minutes*)

Bring the groups back together and emphasize the importance of participants knowing what their values are; then, reflect on how their values are congruent (or incongruent) with the group(s) in which they have membership.

Facilitator Notes   This activity is an important foundational activity. A more robust values identification activity is included in Chapter Five, "Consciousness of Self." (Activity One: Identifying Your Core Value). These two activities can be connected to better illustrate the relationship between values and actions, or can also be facilitated separately. Feel free to add questions that relate specifically to the group participating in this activity. Consider providing the values and mission statement of the organization that the participants are a part of as a way for participants to see how their personal values align or do not align with the organization. It is important for participants to discuss what to do when their personal values come into conflict with one another (such as loyalty and honesty) as well as when they might come into conflict with an organization's values.

Activity Two: Values in Movies

Time: 30 to 45 minutes

Learning Outcomes   Participants will

- Understand how their personal values influence their decision-making.
- Consider how Congruence with values appears in everyday scenarios.

Materials

- Paper and pens
- Board or screen (if not using worksheet)
- Worksheet with questions (if not using board or screen)
- Projector and screen
- Computer/laptop/speakers

Detailed Instructions   Use only one of the movie clips, or all three of them. Below are brief summaries of each movie clip.

Love and Basketball (2000), www.youtube.com/watch?v=rvv5qjmF2nM
(Length: *2:49 minutes*)
This scene involves the two main characters, Monica and Quincy, meeting up. The characters are in a dating relationship and have been friends since childhood. Both Monica and Quincy are accomplished basketball players and play on their college teams. Monica's focus on her basketball career has caused Quincy to feel neglected and lonely. In this scene, the two have a conversation about their relationship. They both say they value the relationship but neither has made appropriate time for it. The question of Congruence of values comes up for both of them.

Mean Girls (2004), www.youtube.com/watch?v=sT8wMBeVffk
(Length: *2:00 minutes*)
In this scene, you see three of the main characters, Cady, Janis, and Damian. Janis and Damian are coming back from Janis's art show and discover that Cady had a party but did not invite them to attend it. In addition, Cady told Janis she could not attend the art show because of a trip with her parents, which was not the case. Janis and Damian are supposed to be close friends of Cady and are hurt that she chose her new and more popular friends over them. Cady assures Damian and Janis that she values their friendship, but her actions do not demonstrate this to be true.

Frozen (2013), www.youtube.com/watch?v=iSwL2GbRy4g
(Length: *3:44 minutes*)
In this scene, Anna and Kristoff are reunited. However, from afar Anna sees her sister Elsa about to be killed by Hans. Anna immediately leaves Kristoff to go and save Elsa. Anna blocks the sword that would have killed Elsa and is frozen. Elsa is devastated that her sister appears to have died. Elsa hugs her sister and Anna becomes unfrozen. Anna's selfless act was true love.

Have participants answer the following questions silently. Give them 5 to 10 minutes to complete this task. You can have the questions on a worksheet or displayed on a board or screen for everyone to see.

- What values were evident in the movie clip(s)?
- Were the characters' actions congruent or incongruent with their espoused values? How so?
- What lessons can you take away from the movie clip(s) regarding congruency of values?

After participants have completed these questions, have them break into small groups of 3 to 5 people to discuss. Have participants discuss their perspectives with one another.

Bring the groups back together and ask each group to report on the perspectives that were shared in the small groups. Explicitly point out how congruency of values appeared in each of the movie clips. Give opportunity for participants to share other movies or television shows (and if there is time, movie or television clips) where they have seen congruence or incongruence of values.

Facilitator Notes   Facilitators are encouraged to add questions that relate specifically to the group participating in this activity and can substitute the movie clips provided with other relevant movie or television clips.

Activity Three: Sharing Stories

Time: 15 to 30 minutes

Learning Outcomes   Participants will

- Be able to identify the ways in which they have been congruent with their personal values, and find examples when that has not happened.
- Understand how easy it is to have a personal value and not live it out all the time.

Detailed Instructions   Let participants know that this activity will involve reflecting again on their personal values, including instances where it is easy be congruent with their values as well as instances where it is more difficult to be congruent with their values.

   As the facilitator, share examples of a time where it has been easy to be congruent in your values, and ways it has not been. Additionally, you could consider discussing a time when your values came into conflict and how that influenced your ability to be congruent. Some examples are listed below:

- You value the environment and being sustainable, but you use paper towels daily in your home. This could demonstrate incongruence.
- You value being authentic and holistic, but you have two Twitter accounts. Your colleagues do not even know one of the accounts exists. Your professional and personal accounts look like two different people.
- You value giving back to your hometown. You volunteer every month in your hometown community alongside members of that community. This could demonstrate congruence with your values.
- You value obeying the law. You choose not to engage in underage drinking because it is breaking the law. Although there is pressure around you to do so, you resist the urge. This could demonstrate congruence with your values.

- You value helpfulness and trustworthiness. A friend shares information about a new student organization committed to encouraging composting on campus, but asks you not to share information with others until the organization is officially formed. You are also a resident assistant and your building wants to start composting in the near future. You know that your friend's new student organization will be helpful, but you've also been asked to not share that information. How do you remain congruent with your values when they come into conflict?

Have the participants count off by twos or threes to get into small groups. Ask each participant in the small group to share a story of a time when they have been congruent in their values, a time where they have not been, and a time when their values have come into conflict with one another. Remind participants that this is not about feeling guilty or bad, but instead an opportunity for each of them to reflect on how being congruent with our values is difficult and a struggle that is shared by many.

Once each participant has shared in the small group, ask the groups to come back to the large group. Ask for volunteers who want to share their story and/or how they felt going through this activity. As you wrap up, thank the participants for sharing openly and honestly.

Facilitator Notes   Revise or add questions that relate specifically to the group participating in this activity. Remember to affirm people that share in the small group. It might be risky and vulnerable for participants to share their stories, so let them know their effort is acknowledged and appreciated. This activity is also an excellent opportunity to discuss what happens when personal values come into conflict and how the context might have an effect on how individuals live their values.

Activity Four: Scenarios

Time: 15 to 30 minutes in large group, 15 minutes in small groups

Learning Outcomes   Participants will

- Understand how value congruence exists in everyday interactions.
- Apply their knowledge of Congruence to real-world situations.

Materials

- Paper and pens
- Board or screen (if not using worksheet)
- Worksheet with scenarios (if not using board or screen)

Detailed Instructions   Split the participants into groups of 3 to 5 participants. Assign each group a different scenario or assign multiple groups the same scenario depending on the size of the group. Contemporary events in the news may also be good scenarios. Scenarios are listed below; a worksheet or slide deck could be used to share this information:

- *Yik Yak*—Susan is a leader who is well respected in her organization and is considered a role model to her peers. She is a champion for promoting inclusive environments in her organization. Susan constantly speaks up in meetings when offensive remarks are made and challenges her friends to be cognizant of their words and actions. One afternoon, Susan goes out to lunch with friends who are also members of her organization. It is a beautiful spring day and they opt to sit outside to take advantage of the warm weather. Less than a block from the restaurant, a LGBTQ pride parade is taking place. Susan gets on Yik Yak and writes, "Can I have lunch in peace without the rainbow folks parading their sexuality? #getaroom." Malia, one of Susan's friends and a fellow member of her organization, is next to her and sees the hashtag in the last part of the message, "#getaroom." Malia then logs onto Yik Yak to see the entire message and is shocked that her friend Susan would write this. Malia does not say anything in the moment but when they get back to campus, she cannot shake this. Malia is debating confronting Susan on this behavior.

- *Family*—You are attending dinner with your family. Your family gets together one Sunday a month and you are excited to see everyone and catch up. Each family member gives a brief update on what is going on in their life, and what is currently exciting them. You cannot wait to share how you have been working on a campaign to provide women with equal pay to men. You have never thought of yourself as a feminist, but currently feel that title fits nicely. When your turn comes around, you begin explaining your work on this campaign. You explain how excited you are to participate in the democratic process. As you continue sharing, you notice some of your family members rolling their eyes and appearing disengaged. You try to ignore it and continue speaking until your uncle blurts out, "Why do women complain so much? It's not like they have to work if they don't want to. Why even waste your time on this?" You are shocked into silence and leave right after dinner without addressing your uncle or the other family members who were rolling their eyes.

- *Movie*—You love going to the movies. You do not even mind going by yourself as it is a treat for you. Because you look young, the workers at the movie theater charge you the student rate. As a new professional, you do not mind because your salary is not high and you attend movies so often that the discount is appreciated. One afternoon you take your 10-year-old niece with you to the movie theater and when the movie theater worker asks if you are a student and you respond, "Yes," your niece looks confused. Once you both are seated in the theater, your niece asks why you lied. Your niece states, "You always tell me to be honest but you were not honest today." You are not sure how to respond.

After you have assigned the scenarios to each small group, give each group time to discuss the scenarios. Ask participants to pay attention to Congruence and how it shows up in the scenario.

Bring the groups back together and ask each group to share the scenario they investigated and how each group saw Congruence (or incongruence).

Facilitator Notes   Revise or add scenarios that relate specifically to the group participating in this activity, or adapt the scenarios included. Make sure participants connect these scenarios with the nuances associated with Congruence. You might need to make this connection explicit for participants.

Activity Five: Contextualized Me

Time: 30 to 60 minutes

Learning Objectives   Participants will

- Consider personal identities and perceptions of identities in context.
- Discuss the connection of context and congruence.

Materials
- Paper bags
- Markers
- Slips of paper and writing utensils

Detailed Instructions   On the outside of the paper bag, have participants write their name as well as any visible identities and identities that they are comfortable sharing in *any* environment. These could include social identities (see Chapter Five, "Consciousness of Self," Activity Four: Social Identity Exploration for resources and activities related to social identity exploration), and personal identities, such as family roles, employment roles, or affinity groups. Examples of what individuals might write on the outside of their bags include college student, soccer fan, woman, Asian American, tall, SGA president, and youngest sibling.

On the slips of paper, have participants write down invisible identities and identities that they are comfortable sharing only in *certain* environments. These identities could also include social identities and personal identities. Individuals will not be asked to share what is inside of their bags unless they are comfortable doing so. On the back of each slip of paper, participants should indicate particular spaces in which they are comfortable sharing this identity. Examples might include: "I have a learning disability and am comfortable sharing only with my parents"; "I identify as gay and share this only with friends"; or "I am adopted, but only share this with very close friends and family."

After participants are finished filling out their bags and slips, have them get into groups of 2 to 3 people to discuss how this activity made them feel. Was it difficult to consider identities in context? Are there identities they are comfortable sharing in this group that they would not share elsewhere? Does only sharing part of who we are make us incongruent? Why or why not?

Facilitator Notes   Be mindful that the learning environment in and of itself is a contextualized place. Note that participants should only share what they are comfortable sharing, and maintain confidentiality. The purpose of this activity is to highlight how context is important to Congruence.

> Supplemental Readings

Greenleaf, R., Spears, L., Covey, S. & Senge, P. (2002). *Servant leadership: A journey into the nature of legitimate power and greatness.* New York, NY: Paulist Press.

Jones, S. R., Kim, Y. C., & Skendall, K. C. (2012). (Re-)framing authenticity: Considering multiple social identities using autoethnographic and intersectional approaches. *The Journal of Higher Education, 83,* 698–724. doi: 10.1353/jhe.2012.0029

Kraemer, H. (2011). *From values to action: The four principles of values-based leadership.* San Francisco, CA: Jossey-Bass.

Pasque, P. & Nicholson, S. (Eds.). (2011). *Empowering women in higher education and student affairs: Theory, research, narratives, and practice from feminist perspectives.* Sterling, VA: Stylus Publishing.

Schwartz, A. J. (Ed.). (2015). *New Directions for Student Leadership: No. 146. Developing ethical leaders.* San Francisco, CA: Jossey-Bass.

> Media

Sarah Asaftei McDugal (2016, May 6). *Your Core Values are Crucial to Your Leadership* [Video file]. Retrieved from: http://youtube.com/watch?v=UAHTd68MJgQ

"The Only True Leadership is Values-Based Leadership": www.forbes.com/2011/04/26/values-based-leadership.html

Clint Smith (2014, July). TED Talk: The Danger of Silence. Retrieved from: www.ted.com/talks/clint_smith_the_danger_of_silence

Shamika Karikari (2015, June 9). TED Talk: Leading with who we are. Retrieved from: http://youtube.com/watch?v=0d1uaB1NphY

❯ Other Resources

The Journal of Values-Based Leadership (JVBL): www.valuesbasedleadership
journal.com

Journal of College and Character (JCC): www.naspa.org/publications/journals/
journal-of-college-and-character

Values in Action (VIA) *Assessment*: www.viacharacter.org

❯ Suggested Questions for Discussions or Assignments

- Would someone who just met you be able to identify your values by observing your behavior? Do others see you as you see yourself?
- How can the personal values of individual group members contribute to or be transformed into shared group values?
- How do your social identities (e.g., your race, gender, sexual orientation, nationality, religion, ability status, etc.) impact your ability to be congruent or not in various environments? In what situations is it more challenging to be congruent with values?
- How do you deal with an impasse? If several members in a group draw a line in the sand, how do you help to move the group forward without group members feeling like they have to sacrifice their core values?
- Suppose you begin to realize that your fundamental values are in stark opposition to those with whom you are working. How far should you bend for the good of the group? What is the threshold at which you would walk away from the group or project?
- Do you think core values can change? Are they fixed or flexible?
- Examine your social media posts over the past few weeks. To what extent does your online presence align with who you really are? Would a person who does not know you have an accurate perception of who you are and what is important to you based on what they see online?

› Reference

Gehrke, S. J. (2008). Leadership through meaning-making: An empirical exploration of spirituality and leadership in college students. *Journal of College Student Development, 49,* 351–359. doi: 10.1353/csd.0.0014

Shamika N. Karikari is an educator committed to racial justice. She is currently a doctoral student in the Student Affairs in Higher Education (SAHE) program at Miami University and doctoral associate for Career Services. She is dedicated to empowering others to use their voice to bring change to the spaces they occupy. Shamika's extensive work in residence life, academic support, and orientation provided her with opportunities to serve students and support them during their collegiate experience. She received her B.A. in History from Bowling Green State University and a M.S. in SAHE from Miami University.

Chapter 7

⌄

Commitment

Suresh Mudragada

◇

› Summary of the Key Concepts

The third Individual level value in the Social Change Model (SCM) of Leadership Development is Commitment. Commitment is described as the passion from oneself that enacts action. This passion must come from deep within an individual and thus varies from person to person. It's not about the talent of an individual, but more about how they identify their passions and act on them with perseverance (Duckworth, 2016).

By honing the other Individual level C values of Consciousness of Self and Congruence, Commitment initiates action. Without this action, social change would not be possible. Commitment requires significant engagement and investment of oneself in the intended outcomes of the Commitment (Higher Education Research Institute [HERI], 1996).

Commitment implies action to initiate some kind of change. It can be accomplished either individually or collaboratively through a group. There are multiple internal and external factors that can have an impact on commitment. Personal experiences can develop one's Commitment through ideas, beliefs, and values, and can show up from involvement on college campuses, in community organizations, and at the local, national, and global levels. An individual's mindset will influence their Commitment. Dweck's (2006) research explores the role of a *fixed mindset* (a belief that certain traits, such as intelligence, are natural abilities and cannot change) and the role of a *growth mindset* (a belief that individuals can grow, change, and continually improve). A growth mindset works well with all aspects of the SCM, especially Commitment as an Individual level value. If one commits to a value, organization, or belief, they can grow and learn to be better. Although Commitment comes from within, external factors have influence. Organizations and groups can create and support an environment that resonates with an individual's passions (Astin, 1996).

In order to help create environments that support the development of Commitment, the challenges of Commitment must be understood. Commitment can be better sustained when an individual is in an affirming environment (Daloz, Keen, Keen, & Parks, 1996). Thus, unsupportive environments, burnout, and poor group dynamics are some of the challenges toward meaningful Commitment. The first challenge of unsupportive environments can be seen as an umbrella challenge that can set up the other challenges. Building supportive environments can be difficult because they can vary depending on an individual's needs. It is important to take into account one's identities and experiences when building environments, because there may be additional obstacles for some individuals to overcome (Steele, 2010). If an environment does not promote self-care, burnout can sometimes occur because an individual is overcommitted and stressed (Chen & Gorski, 2015; Maslach, Schaufeli, & Leiter, 2001). In order for social change to be sustainable, one must commit to taking time for self-care. Environments that are not conducive for supporting group dynamics can be detrimental in working toward social change. Poor group dynamics can cause the group to lose sight of their collective commitment.

Collective commitment is a driving force in group work toward social change. Group Commitment is often a combination of the commitments from the individuals involved. Though a group may share a common purpose, individuals have the power to affect the functioning of that group. Individuals can share the same commitment but execute it in different ways. When one's commitment falters, it impacts the rest of the group as well.

Thus, it is imperative that groups understand where its members are coming from, set shared expectations, and build trust in order to better work together for social change.

Supportive Research Findings

Astin and Astin (2000) describe Commitment as what motivates the individual and provides the passion to sustain collective action. Commitment can be demonstrated in a variety of ways, especially related to the content and focus of the values, thoughts, and behaviors of the individual or group (Daloz et al., 1996). Guiding individuals through their leadership development can clarify this Commitment. By allowing them to recognize and articulate their passion in relation to their personal values and beliefs, leadership development can allow for greater engagement in larger commitments and more sustainable relationships with others (Komives et al., 2005).

Burnout is an obstacle in sustaining an individual's Commitment (Chen & Gorski, 2015). When an individual's Commitment wanes, it also impacts those around them (Jaffe, Scott, & Tobe, 1994). Building coping techniques allows individuals to develop resiliency in the face of challenges (Seligman, 2011). Duckworth (2016) argues that perseverance and passion for long-term goals, known as *grit*, is what allows individuals to continue striving for their goals even when facing challenges and failures. It's also about approaching passion in the long-term rather than taking a temporary approach.

Activities Overview

Commitment activities focus on providing space for participants to engage in dialogue with each other on their values. They will be challenged to reflect on past experiences and think critically about what impact they've had on who they strive to be. All of the activities in this chapter ask individuals to be vulnerable and to share their experiences. Thus, it is important to set community guidelines for engaging in these learning activities. This can include maintaining confidentiality, providing others with space to share, speaking from one's own experiences, responding with grace when mistakes are made, and taking ownership of mistakes.

The first activity, *Social Change Timeline*, focuses on creating a visual representation of the stories that everyone brings with them. Participants will demonstrate how past experiences inform one's work. Activity Two, *Picture Your Values*, provides a creative outlet to describe individual Commitments and how they can look different for others. It also stresses the importance of being able to effectively communicate goals and how to work with others that see things differently. The third activity, *Commitment Panel*, varies the most and requires the most time and facilitation resources. By organizing a panel of people who speak on how they effectively execute their Commitments, participants will better understand how they can live out their personal values. Activity Four, *Commitment Reflection*, focuses on taking action, asking oneself difficult questions, and building resiliency. The final activity, *Six Word Commitment Memoirs*, asks students to summarize their commitment in a creative, memorable way.

Estimated Time

Activity One: *Social Change Timeline*, 60 minutes

Activity Two: *Picture Your Values*, 50 minutes

Activity Three: *Commitment Panel*, 60 minutes

Activity Four: *Commitment Reflection*, 50 minutes

Activity Five: *Six Word Commitment Memoirs*, 20 minutes

> **Learning Activities**

Activity One: Social Change Timeline[1]

Time: 60 minutes

Learning Outcomes   Participants will

- Be able to reflect on the experiences that have shaped the ways in which they hope to contribute to society.
- Understand what experiences drive other participants in their journeys toward social change, and how the experiences of their peers are similar and different from their own experiences.

Materials
- Large sheets of paper
- Tape
- Pens or Markers
- Sticky notes

Detailed Instructions   Instruct participants to take some time to reflect on experiences that have led them to their commitments and pursuits. Ask participants to think of 3 experiences or moments in history (their personal history, contemporary history, and/or historical events) which have had a large impact on their values and who they are. These moments should give participants a sense of why they are on their current journeys, and thus impact their commitment toward making change.

Facilitators should model this activity and be vulnerable so that others will be willing to go deep as well. Some may share their family's immigrant stories and how family members struggled to make a better life in an unfamiliar place. Others may share stories of personal struggles and the long-term impact it's had on their experiences. Others may share events in contemporary times or history that may have had indirect impact. This could include discoveries, inventions, social movements, and/or government policies that

---

[1] Adapted from: OCA—Asian Pacific American Advocates. (n.d.). AAPI Historic Timeline. Washington, DC: Author. Used with permission.

provided opportunities for education for a family member, or laws that took away rights from people.

To prepare for the session, complete the following:

- Take several large sheets of blank paper and tape them to a wall.
- Draw a horizontal line across the page at the midway point.
- Now add years to the timeline. You can place the years on sticky notes and spread them across the line. Suggested dates include 1600, 1700, 1800, 1900, 1950, and 2000. Leave some space before 1600, and leave larger amounts of space between 1900 through 2000. Make sure to leave space after 2000 as well for contemporary events. Depending on the age of the group, you may want to leave more space in the time period that outlines their birth to the present, to account for personal experiences.

After framing the activity with participants, divide them into groups of 3 to 5 people. Pass out sticky notes and pens or markers. Instruct the small groups to take a pen and 3 sticky notes each. Explain that they will have 3 to 5 minutes to think about and write a past or present event that has had an effect on their values, beliefs, and goals.

Participants can start placing their experiences on the timeline.

Allow participants 5 to 10 minutes to look at what everyone wrote on the timeline, and ask them to think about what stood out to them and what themes they noticed.

Afterwards, have the group share their contributions with their small group, or as a large group.

Discussion Questions   The following discussion questions can be used to guide a debrief of the activity:

- What was it like to do the activity?
- Did you see any common themes in the stories?
- How have some of these experiences shaped who you are today?
- How have these events and experiences guided your passions?

Facilitator Notes   It is important to affirm the stories shared, and to thank participants for sharing. If this is part of an ongoing training, keep the timeline up and tie it into other conversations or maintain it as a visual representation of where this group is from and what brought them to their Commitment(s). Be attentive to the need to follow up with any student who appears to need a check-in or more time to process the activity with you.

Activity 2: Picture Your Values

Time: 50 minutes

Learning Outcomes   Participants will

- Be able to articulate what their passions are and how they relate to social change.
- Consider how others may interpret their values differently from each other.

Materials
- Notepads
- Colored pencils

Detailed Instructions   Since group Commitment is derived from the combination of individuals in a group, taking time to articulate what individual passions are in a group is important. Some participants may share a similar value or passion and interpret it and execute their goals very differently. This activity is a way for participants to visualize what their Commitment looks for them in a creative medium and also see how others may look at it differently.

Have participants sit in a circle. This activity works best in groups of 6 to 8 participants. Give each participant a small notepad of paper and colored pencils. Instruct participants to draw a picture of a value or passion that they hold deeply, something that drives what they do. This can be anything, from an object to a symbol. Give everyone a minute to think about it and then 3 minutes to draw.

Ask participants to pass their notepad clockwise to the person next to them. Everyone now has a minute to write a sentence describing the value on the next page.

After a minute is up, pass the same direction as before and make sure people can only see the page with the sentence that was just written and not the initial drawing. Everyone now should draw a picture of the value described on the next page. Give everyone 90 seconds to complete this step.

Now, instruct everyone to pass the notepad again so that only the second drawing is visible, and write a sentence describing it on the next page. After a minute, continue to pass and alternate between drawing and writing until each notepad returns to its original participant. Remember that only the drawing or sentence just completed should be visible when passed.

Once participants have their original notepads back, instruct them to see the progression of their value. Ask them to think about what they noticed and if anything stood out to them.

Ask participants to share their value and how it progressed with their group.

Discussion Questions   The following discussion questions can be used to guide a debrief of the activity:

- What was it like to do the activity? What was easy? What was hard?
- How did it feel knowing others were describing and drawing your values? How was it to draw and write about the values of others?
- What did you notice when you saw the progression of your values?
- What does this activity tell you about communicating your values?
- How can values or interpretations of values differ between individuals?

Facilitator Notes   Make sure to touch on the importance of clearly articulating your values and what brings them to their work. Sometimes groups are not given all the information they need and must do their best to interpret what they have. Clearly articulating one's values becomes important to be understood accurately. Challenge participants to think about how it would work in a group that has conflicting values. How would they compromise? Would they compromise?

Activity 3: Commitment Panel

Time: 60 minutes

Learning Outcomes   Participants will

- Understand strategies on how to execute their passion and goals.
- Consider the advice they receive from panelists and how to rebound from failure.

Detailed Instructions   Storytelling is a powerful conduit for leadership development. Hearing the stories of those who are living out their commitments can help participants start to see how they may do it themselves. The panel can be focused on a general theme like activism, or a specific topic like social change in law or business. Think about the audience and what topic they would respond to the most. Ask 2 or 3 individuals to participate on the panel, and ask each of them to prepare a 5-minute introduction of themselves and their work. Ask panelists to focus on how they took their passions into action, and to think about the challenges and obstacles they faced in their work. The following are additional guiding questions to consider:

- Ask panelists a question about a time they failed at something. How were they able to recover from that experience? How were they able to overcome their obstacles? What strategies did they use? What grounded them? What support did they have?

  Provide 10 minutes for participants to ask panelists additional questions. Have participants break into small groups of 3–5 participants after the panelists leave and ask the following:
- What resonated with you from the stories shared? What did you find most interesting?
- What didn't resonate with you? Where did you struggle?
- How do the stories shared relate to your own journey toward your goals?
- What is one tangible action that you can accomplish in the coming week to help you execute your Commitment? How will you hold yourself and each other accountable?

Facilitator Notes   If you have a small group, no additional materials are needed other than enough seating. If you have a larger group or participants also need accommodations, make sure to have microphones. If it is difficult to find panelists, another option is to find some talks online. Look in the resources section of this chapter for examples. If you have a large audience, you may want to collect questions in advance or use a social media platform to collect questions virtually. Depending on your context, panelists might be alumni of your institution, local or campus leaders, or upper-class students whose proximal age to your students may make a big impact. Panelists may also be brought into the space via free conferencing formats. Be sure to brief panelists on the goals of the activity and select panelists that you know will be forthcoming and mindful of their experience. This activity is similar in delivery to *Activity Three: Citizenship for Social Change Panel* in Chapter Eleven, "Citizenship," and might be combined if desired.

Activity 4: Commitment Reflection

Time: 50 minutes

Learning Outcomes   Participants will

- Be able to reflect on their challenges and recognize the similar and different experiences that others have.
- Understand coping techniques and how to build resilience.

Materials
- 6 sheets of easel paper to stick to wall surface
- Enough markers for all participants
- 6 sticky notes per participant

Detailed Instructions   This activity tends to work better in groups of 20 to 30 people. Participants will reflect on questions to understand what motivates their passions and what they struggle with in accomplishing their goals.

Place large easel paper around the room labeled with the following questions:

- What do you value the most?
- What is the best piece of advice you received?
- What is your Commitment?
- What do you struggle with?
- What is something you wish someone had told you?
- What are you most proud of?

Provide participants with 6 sticky notes each (1 for each question), and give them 5 to 8 minutes to reflect and answer the questions listed on the easel paper. Once they have finished writing, have participants place their responses on the corresponding easel paper. Ask participants to take up to 10 minutes to look at the responses in silence. Ask them to split into groups of 6 to 8 people to discuss the following questions for the next 15 minutes:

- Why do you think we did this activity?
- What commonality did you see in the responses?
- What did you expect the responses to look like?
- Why is it important to talk about struggle?
- What has helped you overcome struggle in the past?

Bring the groups back together to report on their conversations. Focus the conversation on how everyone faces obstacles and struggles at times, and how it is not the same for everyone. Spend some time talking about what helped participants overcome obstacles. Note that obstacles are not the same for everyone and even if they are similar, the same solution may not work for everyone the same way. Conversation points should include self-care, having a growth mindset (Dweck, 2006), and that it is okay to ask for help. Wrap up the conversation with any additional tips for building resiliency that were not already covered during the discussion.

Facilitator Notes   Play close attention to themes that come up, as they can help inform additional training or services needed for the population participating or for the whole organization. Oftentimes participants will realize that others are going through or have gone through similar struggles. This may be a good time to bring in resources on having a growth mindset (Dweck, 2006), grit (Duckworth, 2016), activist burnout (Chen & Gorski, 2015), and positive psychology (Seligman, 2011).

Activity 5: Six Word Commitment Memoirs[2]

Time: 20 minutes

Learning Outcomes   Participants will

- Develop memorable mottos that reflect their personal commitments.
- Clarify for others what is most important to them.

Materials
- Paper
- Writing utensils

Detailed Instructions   Ask participants to consider their values, commitments, personal histories, personal passions, struggles, support systems, and so on. (If activities from this chapter are conducted in order, they all connect to these topics.)

Challenge them to summarize all this information into a six-word (no more, no less) Commitment memoir (or statement or credo) that is memorable, true, and represents their personal Commitment. This can be about a particular topic or a particular way they want to engage. Here are some examples:

- "Man to moon, back again, safely." (John F. Kennedy in six words)
- "Can't. Won't. STOP! Must. Today."
- "PTSD: There is no off switch."

---

[2] Used with permission of Six-Word Memoirs from *SMITH Magazine*: http://sixwordmemoirs.com. Connect on social media: Twitter: @sixwords | Facebook: @sixwordmemoirs | Instagram: @sixwordselfie

- "Love, one cookie at a time."
- "People Planet Profit. Triple Bottom Line."
- "Make waves, but avoid the splash zone!"
- "Smiles: gifts not given for all."
- "Muzzles belong on animals, not people."

Give participants 10 minutes to write their Commitment memoir statements. Then, ask them to share with the larger group (or in smaller groups), and encourage others to ask questions. For instance, what words did they struggle with? Did they struggle or was it easy? How does the memoir represent them?

Facilitator Notes   This activity is easily adapted to meet other leadership program needs. The six-word framework can be used to write about most memorable leadership lessons, powerful experiences that have shaped values, advice participants would give to other leaders, mottos for student organizations, and so on.

> Supplemental Readings

Brown, B. (2010). *The gifts of imperfection: Let go of who you think you're supposed to be and embrace who you are.* Center City, MN: Hazelden.

Brown, B. (2012). *Daring greatly: How the courage to be vulnerable transforms the way we live, love, parent, and lead.* New York, NY: Gotham Books.

Brown, B. (2015). *Rising strong.* London, England: Vermillion.

Chen, C. W., & Gorski, P.C. (2015). Burnout in social justice and human rights activists: Symptoms, causes, and implications. *Journal of Human Rights Practice, 0,* 1–25. doi: 10.1093/jhuman/huv011.

Duckworth, A. (2016). *Grit: The power of passion and perseverance.* London, England: Vermillion.

Dweck, C. S. (2006). *Mindset: The new psychology of success.* New York, NY: Random House.

Seligman, M. E. (2011). *Flourish: A visionary new understanding of happiness and well-being.* New York, NY: Free Press.

> Media

Eduardo Briceno (2012, November 18). TEDx Talk: The power of belief: Mindset and success. Retrieved from: http://youtube.com/watch?v=pN34FNbOKXc

Heidi Renner (2014, March 12). TEDx Talk: How Commitment Shapes Our Lives. Retrieved from: http://youtube.com/watch?v=lKE_ebex2tk

Shonda Rhimes (2016 February). TED Talk: My year of saying yes to everything. Retrieved from: www.ted.com/talks/shonda_rhimes_my_year_of_ saying_yes_to_everything

Collection of additional social change TED Talks: www.ted.com/topics/social+change

> Suggested Questions for Discussions or Assignments

- How is the individual value of Commitment related to the other individual values of Consciousness of Self and Congruence? How do these values affect and intersect each other?
- Where does Commitment come from? How can sources of personal Commitment be identified to enhance individual and group performance and socially responsible leadership?
- What are some common barriers to Commitment? How might these be resolved or overcome?
- Take a moment to consider your own personal commitments. In general, what motivates you? (Examples include helping others, recognition, money, making an impact, and so on.)
- Think of times when you have felt most focused, energized, or satisfied. List the experiences that brought you this feeling. Are there themes that run across these examples?
- What do you do to combat burnout and build resilience? What actions have you taken to reflect upon your purpose?

> References

Astin, A. W., & Astin, H. S. (2000). *Leadership reconsidered: Engaging higher education in social change.* Battle Creek, MI: W. K. Kellogg Foundation.

Astin, H. S. (1996, July/August). Leadership for social change. *About Campus, 1*(3), 4–10. doi: 10.1002/abc.6190010302

Chen, C. W., & Gorski, P.C. (2015). Burnout in social justice and human rights activists: Symptoms, causes, and implications. *Journal of Human Rights Practice, 0*, 1–25. doi: 10.1093/jhuman/huv011.

Daloz, L. A., Keen, C. H., Keen, J. P., & Parks, S. D. (1996). *Common fire: Lives of commitment in a complex world*. Boston, MA: Beacon Press.

Duckworth, A. (2016). *Grit: The power of passion and perseverance*. London, England: Vermillion.

Dweck, C. S. (2006). *Mindset: The new psychology of success*. New York, NY: Random House.

Higher Education Research Institute (HERI). (1996). *A social change model of leadership development (Version III)*. Los Angeles: University of California Los Angeles, Higher Education Research Institute.

Jaffe, D. T., Scott, C. D., & Tobe, G. R. (1994). *Rekindling commitment: How to revitalize yourself, your work, and your organization*. San Francisco, CA: Jossey-Bass.

Komives, S. R., Owen, J. E., Longerbeam, S., Mainella, F. C., & Osteen, L. (2005). Developing a leadership identity: A grounded theory. *Journal of College Student Development, 46*, 593–611. doi: 10.1353/csd.2005.0061

Maslach, C., Schaufeli, W. B., & Leiter, M. P. (2001). Job burnout. *Annual review of psychology, 52*, 397–422. doi: 10.1146/annurev.psych.52.1.397

OCA—Asian Pacific American Advocates. (n.d.). *AAPI Historic Timeline*. Washington, DC: Author.

Seligman, M. E. (2011). *Flourish: A visionary new understanding of happiness and well-being*. New York, NY: Free Press.

Six-Word Memoirs. (n.d.). *SMITH Magazine*. Retrieved from: www.sixwordmemoirs.com

Steele, C. (2010). *Whistling Vivaldi: And other clues to how stereotypes affect us*. New York, NY: W.W. Norton & Company.

Suresh Mudragada serves as the Associate Director of the Center for Identity, Inclusion and Social Change at DePaul University. He is involved with ACPA's Asian Pacific American Network (APAN), and has worked at Macalester College. Suresh earned his bachelor's degree from Auburn University, and received his Master's in Education from Loyola University Chicago.

Chapter 8

Collaboration

Darren E. Pierre

Summary of Key Concepts

Collaboration is a key group value in the Social Change Model (SCM) of Leadership Development. The Ensemble's definition reinforces the importance of relationships, shared responsibility, authority, accountability, and the benefit of multiple perspectives and talents in a group process. Collaboration is about more than just coming together—it is centrally about how people value and relate to each other. It's not just about getting things done together; it involves learning about ourselves and others in the process. Collaboration offers a space where there is not a win, or a loss, but rather a process where individuals build consensus as a group and develop a new framework together that is separate from the ideas of each group member.

To understand Collaboration requires understanding the differences between collaboration, competition, cooperation, and compromise.

Whereas competition is often touted as a way to bring out the best from others, it is actually fashioned to invite one person to do better than another person, rather than doing their own personal best. Competition heightens anxiety and centers on winning, not growth. While Collaboration is based in mutual assistance to achieve shared goals, cooperation is based in mutual assistance to achieve individual goals. Collaboration is rooted in teamwork and partnership. Compromise means giving something up for the greater good, while Collaboration requires hearing and considering other ideas and viewpoints with the goal of expanding or redefining these ideas and viewpoints.

Successful Collaboration can be achieved through building trust, broad-based involvement and group diversity, group purpose and goals, and process. *Building trust* opens the path to communication, but can take time and commitment. It requires group members to put aside preset agendas to engage in exploration, to share ownership for the process, to celebrate successes, and to create powerful, compelling experiences for the group. *Broad involvement* and *group diversity* are both the strength and the challenge of collaboration; they allow us to capitalize on multiple viewpoints through creativity and innovation, but also force the group to grapple with different styles and notions of how the group should function. Clarity of *group purpose* is also essential to collaboration. The most effective teams spend a substantial amount of time exploring and shaping and agreeing on group purpose and mission. Finally, Collaboration relies on *process*. Collaboration is rarely done without some semblance of discourse. Mutually agreed-upon expectations are important to ensure that collaborative efforts take place in the most respectful fashion possible. Throughout the collaborative process trust needs to be fostered, and it is essential participants' voices are heard throughout.

> Activities Overview

The first activity, *The Shift*, seeks to look at one scenario from two different lenses—first, by examining the scenario through a lens based in competition; and then, viewing the same scenario through a lens based in Collaboration. Activity Two, *Who We Are*, asks participants to complete a life-mapping exercise describing important events in their lives, in order to identify the diversity amongst the group. Once those differences are identified, participants look at ways their various identities intersect to form new realms of possibility.

The third activity, *Hot and Cold*, centers on strengthening communication and building trust within a team through an obstacle course experience. Activity Four, *Story Time*, is a progressive story (one part builds on another), designed to illuminate how something new can emerge from collaborative efforts with others.

Activity Five, *Something Old, Something New*, invites participants to think creatively about traditional items we use every day, to illustrate how new ideas and opportunities can germinate through creative, collaborative processes. In the last activity, *The Tower*, participants are asked to construct the tallest freestanding structure they can build using general household items, to simulate the process of working collaboratively toward a common goal.

Estimated Time

Activity One: *The Shift*, 30 to 45 minutes
Activity Two: *Who We Are*, 45 minutes
Activity Three: *Hot and Cold*, 30 minutes
Activity Four: *Story Time*, 45 minutes
Activity Five: *Something Old, Something New*, 20 to 25 minutes
Activity Six: *The Tower*, 35 minutes

> **Learning Activities**

Activity One: The Shift [1]

Time: 30 minutes

Learning Objectives   Participants will

- Strengthen their understanding of the differences between Collaboration and competition.
- Cultivate a stronger ability to work within groups.
- Experience synergy within a group.

Detailed Instructions   Divide the group into 2 teams of approximately 10 participants each. (Adjust the activity as needed, according to the size of the group.) Have groups move to opposite ends of the room. Then, give each group the following instructions.

Each team will have 10 minutes to develop a 2 to 3-minute pitch about the importance of teamwork, which they will present to the other team. Team 1 will approach the planning of this presentation from the standpoint of competition; each person in the team should work individually to argue for their idea to be the one that gets adopted for the group. Team 2 will approach this same activity from the standpoint of Collaboration, meaning that each individual in the team is asked to do their best to work well with others as a group in explaining the concept of teamwork.

After 10 minutes, ask each team to present to the other team. After both teams have presented, lead a debriefing of what the differences were in both approaches. Allow 15 to 20 minutes for debriefing.

Discussion Questions   The following discussion questions can be used to guide a debrief of the activity:

- For both groups, describe the process that you derived to come up with your presentation. What worked, and what didn't work?

---

[1] Adapted from Logan, R. (1995). A natural synergy. *American Journal of Management Development* 1(4), 23–27. doi: 10.1108/13527599510064922. Used with permission. License 3890920389274

- As you listened to the other team describe their process for creating their presentation, what differences did you hear in their process in relation to your own process?
- For those on Team 1, how would you do this activity differently, invoking the values of Collaboration?
- Collaboration brings people together around a vision, values, and shared mission. How will you begin to create spaces for the teams you work with to discuss the central vision, values, and mission of the groups you work alongside?
- For both groups, on a scale of 1 to 10 (1 being poor and 10 being great), how would you rate your group's ability to complete the task at hand? How would you rate your group's process to develop the presentation?

Activity Two: Who We Are

Time: 45 minutes

Learning Objectives   Participants will

- Understand the benefits of diversity in collaborative partnerships.
- Strengthen their ability to talk about difference as a gain in working in groups.
- Further cultivate an appreciation for inclusion.
- Explore the differences between cooperation and Collaboration.

Materials
- Blank paper
- Pens and Markers

Detailed Instructions   There is no set number of participants for this activity, but for groups larger than 10, split participants into 2 groups or more depending on size, ensuring that small groups are no larger than 7 members each.

Give each participant a sheet of paper and 5 to 7 minutes to list out their various identities. Give participants examples, some safe, and some more vulnerable so they can see that this is a challenge by choice activity.

Identities can include categories such as birth order, geographic origin, religion, political affiliation, ability, sexual orientation, and so on.

After participants have listed their identities, ask them to share within their small group to see where the differences are, and ask them to develop three initiatives that support the greater good based on the diversity of their various experiences and identities. Provide an example if necessary. For instance, a group that contains a gay participant and a participant interested in public health might develop an initiative related to blood donation restrictions that discriminate against the LGBT population.

This activity can also be done for groups rather than individuals. For example, take an organization that is focused on healthy living, and take an organization like the Black Student Union. While their interests may seem different, there is a space for collaboration when you dig deeper. For example, the Black Student Union could partner with the Health Advocates Club to combat heart disease (heart disease being a leading cause of death for African-Americans).

Remind participants of the difference between Collaboration and cooperation by speaking to how Collaboration is related to mutual assistance for a *mutual* goal (whereas cooperation is assistance for an *individual* goal).

Discussion Questions Ask each group (or individual) to share the goal they were able to come up with from the group, or from individuals who have experiences and interests different from their own. Ask participants to consider the following questions:

- How do we begin to prompt effective dialogue across difference?
- What made this exercise challenging, and conversely, what made this exercise less difficult for you?
- When you look toward future opportunities to collaborate across difference, what will help you determine the right network (community) to connect with as you move forward toward your purpose?
- What environmental factors need to be in place to allow for greater Collaboration across difference?
- What formal and informal structures can be put into place that allow for diverse perspectives to be offered in an organization?

Close the activity by sharing the following recommendations:

- Clearly define the purpose of the Collaboration.
- Be purposeful in the invitation in how and who to collaborate with, and avoid "collaboration overload"—that is, collaborating for Collaboration's sake without strongly defined intentions.
- Continually assess the strength and areas for growth for yourself (or the group) as it relates to Collaboration.
- Embrace both the formal and informal networks and infrastructures in place that support a collaborative environment.

Facilitator Notes   For more detail on social identities, see Chapter Five, "Consciousness of Self," for *Activity Four: Social Identity Exploration* and additional resources. This activity can also be completed in conjunction with the Consciousness of Self activities. It may also be useful in Citizenship (Chapter Eleven) if discussing groups collaborating to form coalitions for the benefit of the community.

Activity Three: Hot and Cold

Time: 30 minutes

Learning Objectives   Participants will

- Navigate an obstacle course as a team.
- Strengthen their ability to communicate amongst a team.
- Practice collaborating toward a common goal.
- Further illuminate the role competition may play in Collaboration.

Materials
- Cups (1 cup per group; use a small cup to avoid messes)
- Bucket (1 per group, but you may add more if needed)
- Plastic plates (5 to 7, for use as landmines)
- Small plastic "traffic" Cones (4 to 6, for use as landmines)

- Chairs (2 to 3, for as landmines)
- Hula Hoops (1 to 2, for use as lava pits or quicksand)
- Blindfolds (1 per group)
- Masking or Painter's Tape (to make barriers for the obstacle course, if desired)

Detailed Instructions This activity is similar to an obstacle course, so there needs to be enough room for one person to move around with limited distractions (table, chairs, etc). Design a course that participants can move freely through using materials such as plates, cones, and chairs (see *Materials* for full list of suggested materials needed).

Divide the group into teams of 10 to 15 people. Ask each team to designate one member to be the water carrier. Explain the task to the remaining participants while the water carrier stands outside the room (so that they cannot hear the instructions):

The task is for one person (designated by the team) to start blindfolded, and with a cup of water in hand, with the goal to pour that same water into a bucket on the other side of the room. If the water spills before the person reaches the bucket on the other side of the room, the cup will need to be refilled and they will be asked to restart the course from the beginning. If the person touches any obstacles, they must also restart. The task is complete when the person pours the water into the bucket, and returns to their original position in the room and places the empty cup facedown on the floor to signal that they have completed the task.

Give each team 90 seconds to strategize while having the assigned the water carriers continue to stand outside the room. While teams are strategizing, blindfold the participants assigned the water carrier task. Once the directions are given and the participants are blindfolded, announce that landmines have been added to the course. These landmines should not be touched, and if they are touched while a participant is in play, they will have to start from the beginning.

Each time a person restarts, they will have to be verbally guided back to the start while remaining blindfolded, in an effort to keep the course and placement of landmines a secret from the participant. Once the blindfolded participant has successfully completed the task, lead the group in a reflection of the activity.

Discussion Questions:

- For those who were giving directions, what difficulties did you see in your ability to communicate? What strategy did you employ? Did everyone in the group agree on that strategy? Did everyone in the group contribute? Were there ideas that surprised you?
- For the person blindfolded, what was it like receiving the directions from the group? Did you feel safe? Could the group members directing you have done anything more to help you feel safe?
- How did Collaboration support your efforts with this activity? If it is not mentioned, share about how they had to work together on their communication by not talking over each other so that the message could be conveyed clearly. If this did not happen, mention this as a suggestion of how collaborative leadership could have aided their process.
- Did anyone carry a heavier burden to meet the goal than others? Where did that come from?
- This activity was not described with "winning" as the desired outcome. Did you feel pressure to beat the other team in the course anyway? How did that feeling of competition impact your ability to complete the task?

Facilitator Notes   For larger groups or larger rooms, additional materials may be necessary. You may also ask some participants to sit out the activity and observe instead, looking for signs of Collaboration (or non-collaboration). Be sure to ask the observers to comment. Check with the water carrier volunteers to ensure they are comfortable being blindfolded. If not, identify another volunteer.

Activity Four: Story Time

Time: 45 minutes

Learning Outcomes   Participants will

- Examine the importance of the individual as it relates to teams and groups.
- Identify where collaborations take place within groups.
- Become versed in how to contribute to a process or project already under way.

Materials

- Pictures of different objects, animals, people, places, etc. (Have approximately double the number of pictures as the number of participants in the group.)

Detailed Instructions

Place participants in a large circle. Have participants each grab a picture. Inform participants that this is a progressive story, and as they add to the story, they should find a way to incorporate the picture in their addition to the narrative. For example, if the person who starts has a picture of a lion, they may start the story by saying something like, "once there was a powerful lion who lived in the wild … " As each person goes around in the circle, they should each add to the story based on the picture that they have in front of them.

After everyone in the circle has shared their contribution to the story, ask the following processing questions:

- How was this experience?
- Where did you see Collaboration? (This is a great opportunity to reiterate the differences between collaboration and cooperation. In this example, the group had a common goal that they were working toward, by adding on to the story based on their picture.)
- For those who were at the start of the circle, what did you think of the story after hearing it in its entirety? (Look for ways to illustrate how sometimes in Collaboration you have to release a bit of control. For instance, the person who went first had to let go of their thoughts of what the story should be, in order to allow the story to be what it could be.)
- Did anyone feel stuck after hearing the addition before them? Have you experienced a situation before where you had to contribute to someone else's vision? What was that experience like? If you were stuck, did others try and help? How did that feel?
- How do you see this activity relating back to diversity? (Look for ways people share with you about how they each brought diverse perspectives to this activity that strengthen the overall output: the story.)
- How can incorporating diverse voices into the story of the organizations that you lead help strengthen the overall output of those organizations?

Facilitator Notes   If you are in need of stock photos, there are several open source image sites, such as Creative Commons, Shutterstock, or Getty Images, available on the internet.

Activity Five: Something Old, Something New

Time: 20 to 25 minutes

Learning Outcomes   Participants will

- Exercise innovative approaches to working collaboratively.
- Develop a "think outside the box" mindset as it relates to working within groups.
- Examine how working with a common purpose promotes Collaboration.

Materials
- Common household items (such as a fork, straw, coffee filter, adapter plug, mug, cable wire, lightbulb, mason jar, umbrella, dish, marker, book, picture frame, etc.)

Detailed Instructions   Show the larger group some general items such as a fork, straw, lever, glass, coffee filter, or any other general household items. Split the group into smaller groups (with no more than 5 people per group), and ask each group to take each of these traditional items and repurpose them with a new function. Two items can be used in combination, or you can magnify an aspect of an item to support a new function.

　　After 10 minutes, have each group report back on what new purposes they were able to fashion for their traditional household items.

Discussion Questions:
- How was this exercise made easier by working in groups rather than individually?
- How does Collaboration connect with innovation?
- How can you "repurpose" some of the work taking place within your organizations to better support Collaboration?

- In this activity each group had a common purpose, to reimagine the usage for a general household item. What can a Common Purpose do to help facilitate Collaboration within your organization?

Facilitator Notes   This activity can easily be adapted as a creativity-building exercise to help individuals or groups think outside of the box. Each participant or pair can take one item and spend 10 minutes brainstorming all the ways that item could be used. As you work with participants, observe the ways in which you see Collaboration and innovation displayed. If you have many groups, you may compile a bag full of items, and have each group draw out three or four items at random.

Activity Six: The Tower

Time: 35 minutes

Learning Outcomes   Participants will

- Demonstrate teamwork by working together to build the tallest free-standing structure
- Define Collaboration through practice and simulation.
- Identify common challenges to working collaboratively in teams.
- Develop skills that support working with groups toward a common goal.

Materials
- Balloons (20 per group)
- Pipe cleaners (10 per group)
- Masking tape (1 roll per group)

Detailed Instructions   Split the group into smaller groups of 5 to 10 participants. Give each group a pack of 20 balloons, 10 pipe cleaners, and a roll of tape. Assign a person from each group to serve as the "supervisor." The supervisor will not only contribute to the building of the structure, but will also serve as an observer of the process of how the group came to their decisions in building the tallest structure.

Share with the team that the objective is to build the tallest freestanding structure. The team with the tallest structure measured from base to top will be declared the winner. (Please note, the structure cannot be suspended from a high structure such as a stool, chair, chandelier, etc.) Participants will have 10 minutes to complete the activity. Before groups begin, make sure that everyone has a clear understanding of the rules.

After 2 minutes to plan and 10 minutes to actually construct the tower, measure the height of each structure to determine the overall winner. Use the remaining time to debrief the activity with participants.

Discussion Questions:

- For those who served as supervisors, describe the process that your group employed to build the structure.
- Supervisors, what ways did you see participants negotiating to reach the mutual goal?
- What role did the process play in your success or struggle with this activity?
- For those who worked to build the structure, what ways did you feel included in this activity? Were there any ways you felt excluded during this activity?
- What systems are in place within our organizations that inherently exclude or include others?
- Did any groups consider joining forces with another group so that you had double the resources? Do we ever let competition get in the way of innovative sources of collaboration?

Facilitator Notes   This activity is similar in purpose and scope as Activity Two: *Straw Castles* in Chapter Nine: "Common Purpose," so read through both activities and decide which one more closely meets the needs of the group. *Straw Castles* focuses more closely on identifying shared aims and purposes, while this activity is more focused on the process of Collaboration. If appropriate, the activities could be combined. This activity could also be altered to ask participants to create the most stable, modern-looking, or creative structure.

> Supplemental Readings

Chrislip, D., & Larson, C. (1994). *Collaborative leadership: How citizens and civic leaders can make a difference.* San Francisco, CA: Jossey-Bass.

Cross, R., Ernst, C., Assimakopoulos, D., & Ranta, D. (2015). Investing in boundary-spanning collaboration to drive efficiency and innovation. *Organizational Dynamics, 44,* 204–216. doi: 10.1016/j.orgdyn.2015.05.006

Hansen, M. (2009). *Collaboration: How leaders avoid the traps, create unity and reap big results.* Boston, MA: Harvard Business Press.

Huxham, C., & Vangen, S. (2000). Leadership in the shaping and implementation of collaboration agendas: How things happen in a (not quite) joined-up world. *The Academy of Management Journal, 43,* 1159–1175. doi: 10.2307/1556343

Johnson, D. W., & Johnson, F. P. (2012). *Joining together: Group theory and group skills* (11th ed.). Essex, England: Pearson.

Kouzes, J., & Posner, B. (2006). *A leader's legacy.* San Francisco, CA: Jossey-Bass.

O'Leary, R., Bingham, L. B., & Choi, Y. (2010). Teaching collaborative leadership: Ideas and lessons for the field. *Journal of Public Affairs Education, 16,* 565–592. Retrieved from: www.jstor.org/stable/20790766

> Media

Ken Blanchard (2012, December 27). TEDx Talk: Collaboration - affect/possibility. Retrieved from: www.youtube.com/watch?v=HKGkBRk1kSo

Linda Hill (2014 December). Tedx Talk: How to Manage for Collective Creativity. Retrieved from: www.ted.com/talks/linda_hill_how_to_manage_for_collective_creativity

Groupme: www.groupme.com

Moxtra: www.moxtra.com

Podio: www.podio.com

Slack: www.slack.com

Trello: www.trello.com

> Suggested Questions for Discussions or Assignments

- What limitations can hinder Collaboration? Where are areas within society where Collaboration was given less importance, and what was the result? If Collaboration is a process, what does that process look like for you?

- What are your feelings regarding Collaboration? What things would limit your ability to collaborate with others? Is competition more valued than Collaboration? Why or why not? Identify the ways you have contributed to a collaborative community, and identify the ways you feel you may have limited the process.
- Groups that function well with a strong sense of Collaboration can sometimes be rare to find. How as a group do we know if we are collaborating effectively? What is needed for spaces to be safe in order for people to share openly about what is and is not working in the group?
- Trust is a critical piece in the Collaboration puzzle. What challenges do groups face that compromise trust?
- Reflect on your experiences interacting in multicultural groups. How do your identities, values, and perspectives influence the way you interact with others from different backgrounds? Have you ever felt your voice or perspective was marginalized? Have you ever gotten the sense that someone else in the group didn't feel comfortable sharing?
- Try to think of an instance when a different perspective helped shed light on a challenging situation. What were the conditions that made that contribution possible? What was the environment like? What are some things that you can personally do in a group setting that would enable each group member to bring their full self (talents, perspectives, and identities) to the conversation?
- Think of a group that you are a part of. What are some things that you can personally do to help establish and maintain trust within the group?

› Reference

Logan, R. (1995). A natural synergy. *American Journal of Management Development*, *1*(4), 23–27. doi: 10.1108/13527599510064922

Darren E. Pierre serves as the associate director of Student Activities and Co-Curricular Advising at the University of Chicago, and is a part-time faculty member at Loyola University Chicago. Darren recently published the book, *The Invitation to Love: Recognizing the Gift Despite Pain, Fear, and Resistance.* Darren's research largely centers on understanding the transformative power that derives from people having the courage to live out their truth. He has spoken across the United States on the ideals of integrity, authenticity, and living a life of purpose. Darren earned his Ph.D. at the University of Georgia in college student counseling and personnel services.

Chapter 9

Common Purpose

Kristen A. Rupert

> ## Summary of the Key Concepts

This chapter looks at the value of Common Purpose, which is a Group value in the Social Change Model (SCM) of Leadership Development. Common Purpose serves as a central tenet in understanding group or team values. It gives participants a place to analyze what is working in a group and uses shared values, vision, and aims in order to discern the group's intended goal or outcome. Understanding Common Purpose empowers the group to participate in a shared analysis of the issues at hand or the task to be undertaken. It allows group members to engage in the shared vision for the group or to collaboratively create a vision, and goals and outcomes for that vision.

In understanding Common Purpose it is imperative to remember that buy-in of group members is key, especially when articulating the group's common purpose. The transmission of a group's core values to present and future members is essential to the leadership process, and can engender continued enthusiasm when activities are intrinsically rewarding and appropriate to the level of participants; when participants can contribute; and when there are positive external benefits for engagement. It is also important to note that although Common Purpose is central in helping groups function, it does not exist alone and is deeply intertwined with the other C values within the Social Change Model.

Activities Overview

The activities in this section are designed to engage participants in group simulations and discussions around the key tenets of Common Purpose including active listening; shared values, vision, and aims; the occurrence of Common Purpose within groups; and the role of Common Purpose when working in a community of diverse individuals. The first activity, *Telling Tales*, emphasizes the importance of active listening and communication in group development, and provides a foundation for the other group activities in this chapter. Activity Two, *Straw Castles*, engages participants in a simulation that illustrates the missed opportunities when individual efforts supersede shared aims. Activity Three, *Metaphors and Similes*, helps participants consider how they conceptualize their group and make meaning of others' beliefs about the group. The fourth activity, *Diving Deeper into Visions/Values*, challenges participants to reconcile differences in ideas of group purpose. Activity Five, *Finding Your Purpose and Adapting Your Purpose*, focuses on identifying the purpose of a company and how purpose can be adapted, and asks participants to identify other examples of adapted purpose. Finally, Activity Six, *Personalized vs. Socialized Vision and Decisions*, asks a group to consider specific past decisions and discuss how they were made.

Estimated Time

Activity One: *Telling Tales*, 45 minutes

Activity Two: *Straw Castles*, 30-minute activity, 10-minute discussion

Activity Three: *Metaphors and Similes*, 20 minutes

Activity Four: *Diving Deeper into Visions/Values*, 30 minute activity, 60-minute discussion

Activity Five: *Finding Your Purpose and Adapting Your Purpose*, 3-minute video, 10-minute discussion, 20-minute activity

Activity Six: *Personalized vs. Socialized Vision and Decisions*, 30 to 40 minutes

❯ Learning Activities

Activity One: Telling Tales[1]

Time: 45 minutes

Learning Outcomes   Participants will

- Practice active listening skills.
- Understand the connection between active listening, communication, and Common Purpose.

Materials
- Writing utensils (1 per participant)
- Paper (1 piece of paper per participant)

Detailed Instructions   Active listening and communication are important skills that help develop a group's Common Purpose. Have participants form a circle and give them the following instructions:

Your task is to tell a story as a group. In order to do so, you must focus on the person speaking and listen to the words the person says. It is important that you focus on listening, rather than identifying what you might say in response. To accomplish this task, one person will start the story with a sentence. The person who starts may speak for as long as they desire. Anyone in the group may add to the story at any time by clapping their hands, which indicates to the person speaking that it is time to yield to the person who clapped. You have 15 minutes to develop your story. Once your group has told their story orally, you will each be asked to write a synopsis of the story you heard.

Once the group has told their story, ask each person to spend 5 minutes writing their synopsis of the story that was told. After they are done, have participants get into pairs or small groups to compare their synopsis for about 10 minutes. Finally, ask a few pairs or groups to share in a debrief of the exercise.

---

[1] Developed by Kristan Cilente Skendall

Discussion Questions   The following discussion questions can be used to guide a debrief of the activity:

- What was the experience like to practice active listening?
- How did your synopsis of the story compare to the rest of your group?
- Why might there be variations in how people remembered and retold the group story?
- Were some synopses filled with too much detail? Were others too broad? Why might that be the case?
- Why are the concepts of active listening and communication important for working in groups and understanding Common Purpose?

Facilitator Notes   This activity works best in groups of 20 participants or fewer. If you have a larger group, you might consider splitting into smaller groups. In debriefing the exercise, it is valuable to integrate the concepts of active listening, social perspective-taking, and good communication skills.

Activity Two: Straw Castles

Time: 40 total minutes (20 minutes for castle construction, 20 minutes for discussion)

Learning Outcomes   Participants will

- Be able to identify how Common Purpose is communicated.
- Identify opportunities where working as a group for shared aims and purpose is more effective than working in separate silos.

Materials
- 200 drinking straws (100 drinking straws per group)
- 2 rolls of scotch or masking tape (1 roll per group)

Detailed Instructions   Seat participants in small groups (a minimum of 2 groups is necessary). Give each group a roll of scotch or masking tape and 100 drinking straws. Tell the participants that they have 20 minutes to create the biggest castle they can, made out of only the straws and tape. Participants may ask for clarification at this point, but reinforce that the only rule is that they can only use the tape and straws. Set a timer for 20 minutes and provide time updates every 5 minutes. When time is up, allow the groups to show off their castles and talk about their process for creating their masterpiece.

Discussion Questions   The following discussion questions can be used to guide a 20-minute debriefing of the activity:

- Why didn't you choose to merge with the other group(s) to create a larger castle with more materials? Alternately, what led you to merge with the other group(s)?
- What was the Common Purpose or end goal of the activity? Did you complete the purpose, or did your group assign other outcomes to the activity?
- What would have led your group to be more successful?
- How did your group communicate with one another while working on this activity? Were you collaborative? Did you make decisions by consensus?

Facilitator Notes   For this activity it is important *not* to tell participants this is a game or a competition, even though they may make that assumption. The aim of the activity is to get participants to think about merging their groups or working together to complete the activity outside of the silo of their small groups. Do not worry if this does not happen; it provides a good starting place for discussion around Collaboration and Common Purpose after the activity.

This activity is similar in purpose and scope as *Activity Six: The Tower* in Chapter Eight: "Collaboration," so read both activities and decide which one more closely meets the needs of the group. This activity focuses more closely on identifying shared aims, while *The Tower* is more focused on the process of Collaboration. If appropriate, the activities could be combined.

Activity Three: Metaphors and Similes[2]

Time: 20 minutes

Learning Outcomes   Participants will

- Explore individual conceptualizations of the group in a creative fashion.

Detailed Instructions   Have each participant think of a metaphor (a comparison to illustrate a concept) or simile (an explicit comparison to illustrate a concept that traditionally uses "like" or "as" to do so) that represents the group. Some examples are listed below:

- "A car is representative of our group. Each person represents a different component of the vehicle and collectively we keep moving."
- "A band can be used to describe our group. Each person represents an instrument that sounds good independently, but together creates music."
- "Our group is like a tree, because we are rooted in our values and we are constantly growing."
- "Our group is like a postcard, because we are always trying to convey a lot of information in a little bit of time, and appearances are important to us."
- "Our group is like a boxing glove—we look soft on the outside, but we hit hard when crossed."

Once each participant has their simile or metaphor written, have them share it with the group, or write/draw it for the others to see. Process the exercise with the participants using the following processing questions:

- Were there any themes to the metaphors and similes you shared? Did they seem mostly positive or negative? Were they mostly about something specific (such as how decisions are made, how group members interact,

---

[2] Adapted from Teh, A., & Ostick, D. T. (2010). Common purpose. In W. Wagner, D. T. Ostick, S. R. Komives, & Associates (Eds.). *Leadership for a better world: Instructor manual* (pp. 105–117). A publication of the National Clearinghouse for Leadership Programs. San Francisco, CA: Jossey-Bass.

or the group's purpose)? What does this tell you about the group's energy?

- Were there any similes or metaphors that you did not agree with? Why is your conception of the group so different from other individuals? What similes or metaphors seemed correct to you?
- Were you happy with the metaphors and similes? What metaphors and similes would you *like* the group to be seen as by its members?

Facilitator Notes   This activity works best for an intact group, though it could be modified to work for forming groups or randomly assigned groups by assigning mock mission statements to a small group, or giving groups example companies to use as a guide.

Activity Four: Diving Deeper into Visions/Values

Time: 90 minutes, 10 minutes for introduction, 40 minutes in small groups, and 40 minutes in the large group

Learning Outcomes   Participants will

- Be able to identify values of their group and create a vision for their group.
- Consider how consensus may help or hinder a group when trying to find a Common Purpose.

Materials
- Large sticky flip chart paper (or tape and flip chart paper)
- Markers

Detailed Instructions   Instruct the group that part of Common Purpose is having a shared vision and shared values. Before beginning the activity, take a few minutes to discuss the idea of consensus and what that means to a group. Explain to the group that consensus does not necessarily mean that everyone is satisfied with the decision or that even most group members believe that the best decision has been reached. A consensus is present when all team members have had the opportunity to voice their concerns and are comfortable enough with the decision to support its implementation (Rayner, 1996). The facilitator can also use the four guidelines of consensus (Rayner, 1996, p. 76 as cited in Drechsler Sharp & Teh, 2016) to help guide the group.

Four guidelines for reaching consensus within a group:

1. Clearly define the issue facing the team
2. Focus on similarities between positions
3. Ensure that there is adequate time for discussion
4. Avoid conflict-reducing tendencies. (For example: taking a vote)

Split the large group in half (or into smaller subgroups). Ask each subgroup to write on flip chart paper what they believe the vision or purpose of the organization is, using *consensus*. Once complete, each subgroup will then decide on 5 to 10 values they believe best represents the members of the organization, and the organization as a whole. Subgroups should take about 30 minutes to craft their vision and list of values. Once all groups have completed this task, bring the groups together and have them report back on what they determined. After each group has reported, lead a debriefing of the activity with the large group by using the discussion questions that follow.

After the first discussion, ask the participants to complete the same activity again, but this time as a large group. In addition, ask participants to come to a consensus on their decisions about the vision and values.

Discussion Questions   The following discussion questions can be used to guide a debrief of the activity:

- How did the subgroups come up with their vision and values?
- Did more than one group share similar values? Did those values (or words used) mean the same thing to all groups?

- What happens if a value means something to one group but something different to others? How do we communicate our values clearly, ensuring that those values indicate the same purpose or idea to each group member?
- When comparing visions did you see similarities? What were they? Do any of the visions contradict other groups' visions?

Facilitator Notes   This activity works best for an intact group, but could be modified for a forming group. If participants are struggling to name values for their organization you can have them look up a values list online to use in conjunction with a values activity from Chapter Five (*Consciousness of Self*) such as *Activity Four: Social Identity Exploration* or Chapter Six (*Congruence*) such as *Activity One: My Values* or *Activity Two: Values in Movies*.

Activity Five: Finding Your Purpose and Adapting Your Purpose

Time: 35 minutes

Learning Outcomes   Participants will

- Be able to clearly identify an organization's purpose/vision.
- Analyze reasons a company/organization may have for adapting their vision/purpose.
- Consider the impact on people of changing or adopting the vision/purpose of the company/organization.

Materials
- Online TOMS video: vimeo.com/79833962; Length: 3:14 minutes, and equipment for viewing
- Computers, tablets, or devices to access the internet
- Flip chart paper
- Markers

Detailed Instructions   Begin this activity by asking participants what they know about the company TOMS. After gathering responses, play the short TOMS video. Then, ask for responses based on the following questions:

- What was TOMS's original vision/purpose?
- How did the company adapt their vision/purpose when they received criticism?
- Did they only adapt once or was adapting a longer process?
- What was the impact of change on how they do business?
- Is feedback necessary for growth and change?
- Do you think it is difficult to change the vision/purpose of your organization?
- Did the organization grow or get better after they adapted?

Once participants have completed the discussion questions split them into small groups of 2 to 3 participants and give them the following *prompt*:

"Use the internet to find an organization or company that has had to adapt or shift their vision/purpose since their creation. Use the flip chart paper provided to answer the following questions:

- What was the company or organization's original vision/purpose?
- What is their new vision/purpose?
- What took place that caused them to make changes?
- Are they a better company now than they were before?
- What was the impact of adapting the vision/purpose on the company or organization?
- What are the espoused values of the organization? What are the organization's enacted values?"

When participants are finished, have them regroup and share their findings.

Facilitator Notes   If participants are having trouble thinking of companies or organizations, direct them to think about how due to changing society, technology or human needs organizations/companies may have had to adapt to keep up. IBM and Xerox are good examples of this due to changing technology. Häagen-Dazs is another great example of a company that needed to adapt when environmental challenges threatened its business. Dweck's (2006) research on mindset also offers useful examples for this activity.

While not necessary for participants to read, it might be helpful for the facilitator to learn more about TOMS shoes and criticisms in case participants need more context. There are many articles online, but this one by Joshua Keating (2013) gives a balanced perspective: www.slate.me/ 1jHrlRu.

Activity Six: Personalized vs. Socialized Vision and Decisions[3]

Time: 30 to 40 minutes

Learning Outcomes   Participants will

- Analyze past group actions to understand how decisions are made in the group.

Detailed Instructions   Remind the group of the difference between personalized and socialized decisions (Drechsler Sharp & Teh, 2016; Howell, 1988):

- *Personalized*—when a person in charge comes up with the vision, plan, or idea, and then passes it on to others in the group.
- *Socialized*—when group members contribute to setting the broader direction for the group.

Have the group as a whole brainstorm the last 10 decisions that were made regarding the group. (This is left purposely broad to avoid tipping the balance to decisions made by the *group*, versus decisions made by the *positional leaders* of the group.) Using the list of ways that decisions are made in a group, ask the group to place each decision under a category.

---

[3] Adapted from Teh, A., & Ostick, D. T. (2010). Common purpose. In W. Wagner, D. T. Ostick, S. R. Komives, & Associates (Eds.). *Leadership for a better world: Instructor manual* (pp. 105–117). A publication of the National Clearinghouse for Leadership Programs. San Francisco, CA: Jossey-Bass.

Categories include the following (Drechsler Sharp & Teh, 2016; Johnson & Johnson, 2013):

- *Decision by authority without discussion*: A single positional leader makes a final decision without consulting group members.
- *Decision by authority after discussion*: The positional leader consults group members for their perspectives and ideas, but ultimately makes the final decision.
- *Expert member*: The final decision is made by the group member who has the most knowledge or experience related to the issue or problem.
- *Average member's opinions*: The decision is based on what is presumed to be the opinion of the most typical member.
- *Majority control*: The decision is based on the opinion held by the majority of the group's members.
- *Minority control*: The decision is made by a few key members, often when the group is dealing with time pressures.
- *Consensus*: Group members continue to discuss and persuade each other until everyone agrees (or those who do not agree are willing to commit to the decision).

Discuss with the group why one category is more common or less common than others. Are individuals comfortable with how decisions are being made in the group? Why or why not? Discuss what decision-making process group members would prefer. How can the group accomplish this?

Discussion Questions   The following discussion questions can be used to guide a debrief of the activity:

- How do you contribute to how decisions are made in the group? Is this helpful or harmful to the group? Do you abdicate visioning and decision-making to others, or control decision-making in the group at the expense of others?

- Ideally, how would you like decisions to be made in your organization? What challenges might be associated with that approach? What would the value of that approach be?

Facilitator Notes   This activity works best for an intact group, but can be modified if the group is still forming or random. To adapt this activity, you might consider using a common social movement or historical movement to categorize decisions made over time.

Supplemental Readings

Astin, A. W., & Astin, H. S. (2000). *Leadership reconsidered: Engaging higher education in social change.* Battle Creek, MI: W.K Kellogg Foundation.

Crosby, B., & Bryson, J. (2005). *Leadership for the common good: Tackling public problems in a shared-power world.* San Francisco, CA: Jossey-Bass.

Kurtzman, J. (2010). *Common purpose: How great leaders get organizations to achieve the extraordinary.* San Francisco, CA: Jossey-Bass.

Haber, P., & Komives, S.R. (2009) Predicting the individual values of the social change model of leadership development: The role of college students' leadership and involvement experiences. *Journal of Leadership Education, 7*(3), 133–166. doi: 10.12806/v7/i3/rf4

Media

This American Life (Producer). (2016, March 11). When *the beasts come marching in* [Audio podcast]. Retrieved from: www.thisamericanlife.org/radio-archives/episode/582/when-the-beasts-come-marching-in

Ed Muzio (2009, March 10). *Group decision-making that works* [video file]. CBS News. Retrieved from: www.bnet.com/2422-13731_23-265796.html

Charlie Harayz (2010, April 1). TEDEd Talk: Drive: The surprising truth about what motivates us. Retrieved from: http://ed.ted.com/featured/LT8oQQTo

Larry Kesslin (2014, February 21). TEDx Talk: Shared common purpose. Retrieved from: www.youtube.com/watch?v=yC3inLuWoyQ

> ## Suggested Questions for Discussions or Assignments

- Why is Common Purpose an important leadership value?
- Some Ensemble members have described Common Purpose as the most challenging value in the Social Change Model. Do you agree? Why or why not?
- Think about a group you are part of. Does it have a Common Purpose? If so, how would you describe the way in which that group arrived at its Common Purpose? If not, what could you do to begin that process?
- A student once observed that a group would never come to agree on a Common Purpose if it could not work collaboratively. Do you think this is true? Why or why not?
- Imagine you are part of a group and cannot tell what its mission or vision is. What evidence or indicators might give you a clue? What questions would you ask to find out?
- Thinking about your own experience, what is the difference between embracing a predefined vision and participating in the formulation of that vision with others?

> ## References

Drechsler Sharp, M., & Teh, A. (2017). Common purpose. In S. R. Komives, W. Wagner, & Associates, *Leadership for a better world* (2nd Ed.; pp. 127–148). San Francisco, CA: Jossey-Bass.

Dweck, C. S. (2006). *Mindset: The new psychology of success.* New York, NY: Random House.

Howell, J. M. (1988). Two faces of charisma: Socialized and personalized leadership in organizations. In J. A. Conger, R. N. Kanungo, & Associates (Eds.), *Charismatic leadership: The elusive factor in organizational effectiveness* (pp. 213–236). San Francisco, CA: Jossey-Bass.

Johnson, D. W., & Johnson, F. P. (2013). *Joining together: Group theory and group skills* (11th ed.). Upper Saddle River, NJ: Pearson Education.

Keating, J. (2013). Is TOMS Shoes Listening to its Critics? *Slate.com.* Retrieved from: www.slate.me/1jHrlRu

Rayner, S. R. (1996). *Team traps: Survival stories and lessons from team disasters, near-misses, mishaps, and other near-death experiences.* New York, NY: Wiley.

Teh, A., & Ostick, D. T. (2010). Common purpose. In W. Wagner, D. T. Ostick, S.R. Komives, & Associates (Eds.). *Leadership for a better world: Instructor manual* (pp. 105–117). A publication of the National Clearinghouse for Leadership Programs. San Francisco, CA: Jossey-Bass.

Kristen A. Rupert is a doctoral student at the University of Maryland, College Park in the Department of Counseling, Higher Education, and Special Education with a focus in student affairs. She also serves as a graduate coordinator for the Leadership Studies Program through the College of Education and the Adele H. Stamp Student Union-Center for Campus Life. Kristen earned her M.Ed. in higher education and student affairs at Kent State University.

Chapter 10

Controversy with Civility

Rian Satterwhite & Christopher Ruiz de Esparza

> Summary of Key Concepts

Controversy with Civility is the third Group level value in the Social Change Model (SCM) of Leadership Development. Conflict is understood to be characterized as "an argumentative environment of power, debate and competition" (Alvarez, 2017, p. 151) where the final outcome is won or lost. By contrast, Controversy with Civility is characterized by a "safe and supportive environment of trust, respect and collaboration" (Alvarez, 2017, p. 151) shaped by mutual inquiry and shared learning. Ultimately, Controversy with Civility challenges participants to discuss diverse perspectives from a place of respect and understanding.

Controversy with Civility is not simple politeness. Rather, practicing it means engaging challenging differences of opinion and experience through dialogue and respect, seeking to ultimately develop a more sophisticated and complex understanding of the topic as well as, in many instances, a satisfactory decision. Engaging with others in this manner is a challenge to do well, and honing this ability is a lifelong practice. Controversy with Civility is therefore as much a shift in thinking (a developmental process) as it is a shift in behavior, though it is likely through behavior—or practice—that the desired development is nurtured.

Boyd (2006) challenges the narrow definition of civility—its "functional role in maintaining the peace and order of society" —in order to position civility as "a moral obligation borne out of an appreciation of human equality" (p. 875) that helps us engage with the "plurality of different beliefs, cultures, and identities" in society (p. 872). This definition links civility with a morality grounded in shared human experience, and situated squarely within a social justice framework. Thus, to truly understand Controversy with Civility means to create a sustained culture and commitment within a group that fosters an inclusive environment and affirms the value and dignity of each participant.

A concept central to this work, and related to Boyd's (2006) framing of civility, is *Social Perspective-Taking (SPT)*, defined by Dugan, Kodama, Correia, and Associates (2013) as "a higher order cognitive skill reflecting the ability to take another person's point of view as well as accurately infer the thoughts and feelings of others" (p. 27). Nurturing SPT is a core pursuit in exposing participants to Controversy with Civility and underscores the developmental nature of this work.

Promoting a group culture that nurtures Controversy with Civility requires several elements, including an "awareness of one's own worldview, awareness of others' worldviews, building trust, acknowledging and engaging with controversy, examining context and spaces, and fostering dialogue." (Alvarez, 2017, p. 157). Trusting the people in the group and trusting the process are key for making Controversy with Civility productive in a group setting. Group members must trust that the other members will respect their opinion, whether or not they agree; and group members must trust that the collective process will help the group arrive at better decisions and increased cohesion.

> Supportive Research Findings

The ability to recognize other perspectives and empathize with others in an attempt to seek understanding facilitates the development and maintenance of social relationships critical to group processes (Galinsky, Ku, & Wang,

2005). Data from one study in the Multi-Institutional Study of Leadership (MSL) found that social perspective-taking had a strong direct effect on group leadership values of Collaboration and Controversy with Civility, in large part because of its relationship with individual leadership values of Consciousness of Self, Congruence, and Commitment (Dugan et al., 2014). The study also found that social perspective-taking served as a critical mediator of development between the individual and group domain. Some students demonstrated an ability to apply individual capacities in a group context directly, but others need to acquire competence with social perspective-taking in order to do so (Dugan, Kodama, Correia, & Associates, 2013, p. 28).

MSL research shows students self-report that Controversy with Civility is typically the least developed of the Social Change Model (SCM) of Leadership Development C values (Dugan & Komives, 2007), a reminder of the importance of facilitating opportunities for learning and growth related to Controversy with Civility.

> Activities Overview

The first activity, *The Messages We Grow Up With*, allows for an exploration of media influences from childhood and the messages embedded within them about conflict. Activity Two, *This I Believe*, is an individual opportunity to reflect on core beliefs that shape personal worldviews through journaling. The third activity, *Exploring Controversy through Four Corners*, is an interactive way to help participants recognize that difference (of opinion, belief, background, experience, etc.) is intimately tied to an individual's identity and the way that they view and engage with the world. Activity Four, *Door-slammers vs. Door-openers*, invites participants to reflect on dialogue "starters" and "stoppers" from their own experience, using these experiences to help inform ways to invite others into difficult dialogues rather than shutting them down or out. The final activity, *Dialogue Practice: Trying It On*, establishes a structured dialogue for participants to practice their skills, providing clear steps and expectations for participants to utilize as they practice.

Estimated Time
Activity One: *The Messages We Grow Up With*, 50 to 60 minutes
Activity Two: *This I Believe*, 20+ minutes
Activity Three: *Exploring Controversy through Four Corners*, 30 minutes
Activity Four: *Door-slammers vs. Door-openers*, 35 minutes
Activity Five: *Cooperative Controversy*, 30 to 50 minutes
Activity Six: *Dialogue Practice: Trying It On*, 80 to 90 minutes

› Learning Activities

Activity One: The Messages We Grow Up With

Time: 50 to 60 minutes

Learning Outcomes   Participants will

- Identify and describe media influences that may have influenced how they were socialized to think about and engage in conflict.
- Understand that the ways in which we are socialized at a young age frequently shape how we approach conflict today.
- Consider the idea that there are frequently deep histories informing the way that individuals interact in groups.

Materials
- Multiple internet access points to online video clips (computers, tablets, or smartphones)
- Children's books (optional)
- Projector and speakers for larger group sharing (optional)

Detailed Instructions   Break participants into small groups of approximately 3 to 5 people, depending on group size and time constraints (each group will need 5 minutes to report back).

Give the groups 15 minutes to find examples of media that convey a message about conflict from their youth. A fun way to facilitate this is to reference online video clips of cartoons and/or other types of media including children's books, toys, prominent news stories from their youth, and so forth. This expanded choice may be particularly important for adult learners. If needed, structure this time further, such as 5 minutes of individual search time and 10 minutes of sharing in groups.

Alert groups at the end of this time to choose 1 example, and have a representative share it with the whole group, and articulate the messages it conveys about conflict. They should also have the representative offer a summary of the approach to conflict that they found most common in the examples shared in the small group.

Allow 5 minutes per small group representative (including transition time and searching for media if you are set up to display it to the whole group) to share their example, the messages it conveys, and a brief summary of the approach to conflict that they found most common across all shared examples in their small group.

Use the remainder of the time to bring the groups together to reflect on the experience by using the following debriefing questions.

Discussion Questions: The following discussion questions can be used to guide a debrief of the activity:

- We are not bound by media messages about conflict, yet we are influenced by them. Share with a partner your own reflections on the sources from your youth that carried embedded messages about conflict.
- Do you find that your own orientation to conflict is consistent with these examples? If so, how do you think these may have shaped your own approach to conflict? If not, what were counter-messages about or experiences with conflict that influenced you?
- Do you recall significant learning experiences about conflict when you were growing up? Share with a partner one such example. Did that example reinforce messages about conflict that you were surrounded by, or cause you to reevaluate such messages?
- How does this activity and reflective discussion shape your approach to Controversy with Civility? Are there ways in which you conflate

conflict with Controversy with Civility that may impede or increase your effectiveness in groups?

Facilitator Notes   With small adjustments, this activity can be adapted for online or asynchronous contexts, and even for individual participants in a coaching environment. The addition of short reflective essays on their learning or written responses to the reflective prompts can quickly create an engaging environment online or provide ways for an individual to process their learning.

Activity Two: This I Believe[1]

Time: 20 minutes

Learning Outcomes   Participants will

- Compose a belief statement that illustrates a core aspect of their worldview.
- Describe the reflective process required to effectively distill their writing.
- Reflect on how personal histories often drive behaviors in ways that are invisible until surfaced.

Materials
- Writing materials (pens/pencils, paper, and/or computers)

Detailed Instructions   Share these prompts (adapted from http://thisibelieve.org/guidelines) to prepare participants to engage in this reflective, written exercise. While it can be done in person, it will likely yield best results if there is an opportunity for participants to return at a later time after several drafts of writing to allow for a distilled statement.

I invite you to write your own statement of personal belief. I understand how challenging this can be—it requires intense self-examination, and you

---

[1] Adapted from A public dialogue about belief—one essay at a time. (n.d.). Retrieved August 4, 2016, from www.thisibelieve.org/guidelines.

may find it difficult to begin. To guide you through this process, I offer these suggestions for how to best tell a story about yourself:

- *Be specific*: Take your belief out of the ether and ground it in the events that have shaped your core values. Consider moments when your belief was formed or tested or changed. Think of your own experiences, work, and family, and share the things you know that no one else does. Your story need not be heartwarming or gut-wrenching—it can even be funny—but it should be real. Make sure your story ties to the essence of your daily life philosophy and the shaping of your beliefs.
- *Be brief*: Your statement should be between 500 and 600 words. That's about 3 minutes when read aloud at your natural pace.
- *Name your belief*: If you can't name it in a sentence or two, your essay might not be about a belief. Also, rather than writing a list, consider focusing on one core belief.
- *Be positive*: Write about what you do believe, not what you don't believe. Avoid statements of religious dogma, preaching, or editorializing.
- *Be personal*: Make your essay about yourself, and speak in the first person. Avoid speaking in the editorial "we." Tell a story from your own life; this is not an opinion piece about social ideals. Write in words and phrases that are comfortable for you to speak. We recommend that you read your essay aloud to yourself several times, and each time edit it and simplify it until you find the words, tone, and story that truly echo your belief and the way you speak.

The following reflective or discussion prompts may be useful, depending on the context of facilitation:

- What was your experience in writing this belief statement? How did you make the choice to write about the belief that you did? How did you make it personal? Was there a story that immediately leapt to mind, or did you find that you needed to really do some reflective thinking to dig up a way to share it?

- How does this particular belief affect the way you show up in group settings?
- How do you anticipate if the belief shared by your partner might affect the way that it shows up in groups?
- Without going through such an exercise with every team you belong to, how do you think you can best utilize this knowledge of how different beliefs shape the way that we experience the world?
- How can this exercise help you show up in groups more effectively? How can this exercise inform how you perceive others in group spaces?

Facilitator Notes If done as an individual activity in a large group and in person, it may be useful to facilitate sharing statements in paired small groups. Disclosing personal belief statements to a large group in person can be challenging (though perhaps appropriate given the correct context), but it is important to be able to engage with others' work and beliefs for this exercise to enhance not only the awareness of one's own belief system but also the existence and value of others.

It is crucial to note that while understanding and clarifying personal beliefs is important, the harder work occurs in the group space when these beliefs are shared with others. It should be the goal of the exercise and debriefing to 1) allow participants to reflect on and articulate their own stories, but also, 2) challenge them to receive, value, and engage with others.

While this activity is framed around "beliefs," it will certainly reflect individual values. It may be helpful to use this activity to aid participants in clarifying value statements from earlier activities in a more personally reflective way. With contentious and harmful societal issues, some participants may not want to be "civil" and may see that term as a way to shut down their anger, rage, or pain. Invite that anger into the process, and lead the group in a discussion of how others can support addressing injustices that may cause pain.

Activity Three: Exploring Controversy through Four Corners

Time: 30 minutes

Learning Outcomes   Participants will

- Evaluate their own personal assumptions, perspectives, and worldviews while increasing their awareness for other's assumptions, perspectives, and worldviews.
- Weigh the difference between facilitating dialogue around difference versus engaging in debate or argument.
- Reflect and identify tools and skills for engaging others with differing points of view to increase mutual understanding.

Materials

- Space for groups to gather in four distinct corners of the room.
- Four signs (Strongly Agree, Agree, Disagree, and Strongly Disagree)
- List of statements. (*Note*: statements most likely to encourage discussion typically do not have one correct or obvious answer—they should elicit nuanced arguments. The following list provides some examples, but others could also be developed based on group, setting, context of conversation, etc.)
  - Life's fair.
  - I am only responsible for myself.
  - How you act in a crisis shows who you really are.
  - Money can't buy happiness.
  - What goes around comes around.
  - The needs of larger society are more important than the needs of the individual.
  - The purpose of schooling is to prepare youth to be good citizens.
  - People learn from their mistakes.
  - You can't depend on anyone else; you can only depend on yourself.
  - Individuals can choose their own destiny; their choices are not dictated or limited by the constraints of society.

- Doing what is right means obeying the law.
- One should always resist unfair laws, no matter the consequences.
- Groups make better decisions than individuals.

Detailed Instructions   Label four corners of the room with signs reading: *Strongly Agree, Agree, Disagree,* and *Strongly Disagree.* Ask the participants to gather in the middle of the room. (Variation: If space is an issue, you can establish an imaginary line down the side of the room, with one end being *Strongly Agree* and the opposite being *Strongly Disagree.*)

Explain the instructions as follows:

The following statements are a few of the axioms people hold to be true in their lives. For each statement, consider the level with which you agree or disagree and move accordingly to that corner of the room.

Read a series of statements that require participants to consider their own thoughts, values, and positions. Each statement should be read aloud one at a time. After each statement, participants should go to one of the four corners of the room, based on their sentiment with the statement. The movement should be brief and quick. After each statement, ask participants to consider how they came to that position, and why they agree or disagree. Ask a few participants (perhaps 1 or 2 from each corner) to offer their rationale for their current position. As volunteers share their rationale, encourage the remaining participants to practice *mindful listening*—noticing their own reactions to potential disagreement and controversy. (Do they find themselves defensive or judging? Remind them to remain open-minded.)

At the end of the exercise, ask participants to discuss their observations based on the group activity with the signs. Potential themes for processing include:

- *The difference between debate and dialogue:* How would participants employ dialogue skills to engage differing points of view and increase mutual understanding?

- *Strategies for reaching shared understanding of an issue*: How would participants work to ensure all perspectives are taken into account?
- *Examining underlying assumptions*: How do our own opinions impact the way we think about problems, and how can other people's thinking improve our understanding of an issue?

Facilitator Notes   There are many ways for debriefing this exercise. Participants can reflect independently by writing their thoughts and reactions, can pair-and-share their reflections with each other, and/or can debrief as a group.

Activity Four: Door-slammers vs. Door-openers[2]

Time: 35 minutes

Learning Outcomes   Participants will

- Explore the power of asking open-ended questions when engaging others.
- Explore and assess types of questions that can open or close conversations.
- Assess the types of questions they have experienced from others and consider how their relative effectiveness affected the outcome of the situation.
- Learn strategies for effectively approaching others with civility and openness.

Detailed Instructions   Explain to participants that some questions, when asked, have the effect of "slamming the door" on the conversation or on the relationship between the conversation's participants. Other questions have the effect of "opening up a door," shedding new light, or making possible new ways of thinking or talking about something.

---

[2] Adapted from and used with permission of How do questions advance dialogue?. (n.d.). Watertown, MA: Public Conversations Project. Retrieved August 04, 2016, from www.publicconversations.org/sites/default/files/sec10.pdf/.

Invite participants to take a few moments to reflect on questions they've been asked in their life. Are there particular ones they would consider "door-slammers"? Invite participants to write these questions down on a piece of paper for 2 minutes. If needed, provide an example to illustrate the difference between a "door-slammer" and a "door-opener":

Door Opener: "I hadn't heard that before. Can you tell me more?"
Door Slammer: "Where did you get that crazy idea from?"

To encourage ongoing reflection, ask participants to form small groups of 3 to 5 participants to take turns sharing their thoughts about what elements of the questions shut them or the conversation down. Allow participants 2 minutes each to share on the characteristics of "door-slamming" questions. (This should take 5 to 10 minutes total, depending on group size.)

Repeat the process for the "door-opener" questions. Invite participants to take a few moments to reflect on questions they've been asked in their life. Are there particular ones they would consider "door-openers"? Then have them spend 2 minutes writing these questions down.

In the same small groups as before, ask participants to take turns sharing what qualities of these questions felt "opening." Again, participants should take turns, for 2 minutes each, sharing characteristics of "door-opening questions." (This should take 5 to 10 minutes total, depending on group size.)

Bring the small groups together into one large group. Begin a 10-minute discussion on the effects that different kinds of questions (or ways of asking the questions) can have on engaging Controversy with Civility.

Facilitator Notes   This activity can be adapted to specific topics or subjects. For example, the group may be considering ways to open dialogue around the topic of privilege and oppression, around international conflicts, or around other hot button issues impacting group members. The framework provided here is intended to be utilized in a way that aligns with the group's interests and needs for learning about effective dialogue.

Activity Five: Cooperative Controversy

Time: 30 to 50 minutes

Learning Outcomes   Participants will

- Consider perspectives other than their own, and allow differing opinions and experiences to increase their understanding and appreciation of others.
- Practice engaging critically with ideas rather than people.

Detailed Instructions   This group exercise is modeled after "cooperative controversy," a cooperative learning method used to study an issue that generates a lot of disagreement (Bucher, 2004). When using this method, consider these guidelines.

- Evaluate ideas, not people.
- Remember: we are all engaged in a shared learning experience.
- Encourage everyone to participate.
- Listen to everyone's ideas, even if you don't agree with them.
- Seek clarity if what someone says is not clear.
- Try to understand all sides of the issue.

Alternatively, you may choose to have the group engage in shaping its own expectations or norms.

Divide the participants into groups of 4 members. Each group will examine the following statement: "*Students who dine solely with members of their own ethnic group and participate in ethnic student organizations and activities contribute to a decline of ethnic relations on a college campus.*"

In each group, participants should follow these steps:

1. 2 participants should advocate support of this statement while the other 2 participants work from a position of disagreement. (*Allow 5 minutes for preparation, and 5 minutes for dialogue.*)

2. Midway through the discussion, ask group members to switch sides and advocate the opposite position. (*5 minutes prep; 5 minutes dialogue*)
3. Encourage the group to try and reach some consensus amongst itself regarding the statement. (*5 minutes*)
4. Have groups report back and share both their conclusions and their observations with the larger group. (*10 to 25 minutes*)

Facilitator Notes Depending on the group and amount of time available, the facilitator may invite the group to come up with their own agreements or conversation guidelines before beginning. The guidelines in this exercise are provided here as a reference and recommendation, and can definitely be expanded on. It is important for the facilitator to be comfortable facilitating dialogue with an understanding of the intersections of identity, power, and privilege, and how they may influence the discussion.

See the "Suggested Questions for Discussion or Assignments" section at the end of this chapter for more questions about perspective-taking and other prompts that could be useful to help in debriefing this exercise.

Activity Six: Dialogue Practice: Trying It On[3]

Time: 80 to 90 minutes

Learning Outcomes Participants will

- Apply their active listening skills to a group dialogue.
- Utilize their own experience to analyze practices that allowed them to feel understood and increased their willingness to engage in deeper conversation.
- Practice setting and implementing group agreements prior to a structured dialogue.
- Analyze the ways in which their behaviors contribute to opening or restricting group dialogue and discussion.

---

[3] Adapted from and used with permission of the Public Conversations Project. (n.d.). Retrieved August 4, 2016, from www.publicconversations.org.

Materials
- Flip chart paper
- Markers (at least 1 marker per group)

Detailed Instructions   Round 1: Reflection and Preparation (*5 to 7 minutes*)

Provide participants with a few minutes to think about the beliefs, issues, and perspectives that they are most passionate about in their life. Ask them to write down which one, if they spoke of it, would help people understand best what they care about.

Ask participants to think for a moment about when they have spoken about this before.

- When has it gone well?
- What did they hold back or restrain that enabled others to hear and understand them?
- What enabled them to listen so that they understood others better?
- What qualities or skills did they call upon, and what did they actively do that enabled this to happen?
- What might they restrain or bring out today that would help create a good conversation?

Round 2: Group Agreements (*5 to 7 minutes*)

Ask participants to sit in circles of up to 8 participants. Invite each group to develop some basic communication agreements for the subsequent discussion and write them on a piece of flip chart paper.

Round 3a: Opening Questions (*20 minutes*)

Ask one participant to read the following *prompt* aloud for the group:

Briefly name the belief, issue, or perspective that you are passionate about and tell the group about an experience you've had that would help them understand why you feel as strongly as you do. What is at the heart to the matter for you about this?

Allow the group to pause for approximately 2 to 3 minutes as each participant considers their responses. Encourage participants to take notes on what they might want to say and share with the group.

Instruct the group to go around the circle, one at a time, with each person responding to the opening questions for no more than 2 to 3 minutes each. Ask the group to pass the responsibility for staying on time from person to person. As participants share, the remaining group members are silently listening; there should be no questions or comments during this time. Instruct them to take notes as they are listening on the following key points:

- What do they want to especially remember?
- What are some keywords they heard?
- What are they curious to learn more about? What questions might they want to ask later?

Round 3b: Follow-up Questions (*25 minutes*)

After each participant has had the chance to share in Round 3a, instruct participants to take a few minutes and look over the notes they've written about what others have shared. Encourage them to let the stories they've heard sink in, and let the most urgent questions arise from their notes.

- What do they want to know more about?
- What assumptions might they need to check out?

Encourage the group to recall the group agreements established in Round 2. Provide groups 20 minutes to ask follow-up questions and respond to questions. Encourage participants to avoid questions that could potentially start conflict or debate, and instead use questions that allow the speaker to expand on what they have already shared.

Instruct groups to aim for "shared airtime" so that as many people get a chance to ask and respond to questions as possible. Encourage groups to retain self-awareness, other-awareness, and group-awareness throughout the discussion.

Round 4: Reflection and Closing (*20 minutes*)

Provide participants with a few minutes to think about what they experienced in the Round 3 discussion. Use the following *prompts*:

What have you done—or refrained from doing—that led to the exchange going as it did? What else do you want to say to bring this time to a meaningful close for you?

Invite them to write down any notes on their reflections.

After allowing 2 to 3 minutes for reflection, instruct the groups to go around the circle and respond aloud to these prompts, keeping their thoughts brief.

Once each group has completed their internal sharing, bring all the groups together for a closing debriefing of the exercise. Engage participants in a discussion about their experience, and their emerging understanding of how the tools and techniques of dialogue might apply to approaching Controversy with Civility.

Facilitator Notes   This activity specifically includes a segment on establishing group agreements, an essential dialogue component that is often referenced but rarely given any intentional instruction or analysis. Timing may need to be adjusted to include a broader discussion on setting group agreements if this is a new concept for participants. See Arao and Clemens (2013) for a critical examination and reframing of common ground rules used in difficult dialogues.

If you have participants who are unsure of their passions or don't have issues they are compelled about, ask them to think of an issue they have worked on in the past, or to think of a person they admire and an issue that person was passionate about.

❯ Supplemental Readings

Bennett, M. J. (2013). *Basic concepts of intercultural communication: Paradigms, principles, and practices* (2nd ed.). Boston, MA: Intercultural Press.

Brown, J., & Isaacs, D. (2005). *The world cafe: Shaping our futures through conversations that matter*. San Francisco, CA: Berrett Koehler.

Bucher, R. D. (2014). *Diversity consciousness: Opening our minds to people, cultures, and opportunities* (4th ed.). Upper Saddle River, NJ: Pearson Prentice Hall.

Forni, P. M. (2003). *Choosing civility: The twenty-five rules of considerate conduct*. New York, NY: St. Martin's Press.

Gehlbach, H., & Brinkworth, M. (2012). The social perspective taking process: Strategies and sources of evidence in taking another's perspective. *Teachers College Record, 114*(1), 1–29. Retrieved from: http://wangresearch.pitt.edu/wp-content/uploads/2015/04/The-social-perspective-taking-process-what-motivates-individuals-to-take-anothers-perspective1.pdf

Guthrie, K. L., Bertrand Jones, T., & Osteen, L. (2016). *New Directions for Student Leadership: No. 152. Developing culturally relevant leadership learning*. San Francisco, CA: Jossey-Bass.

Katzenbach, J. R., & Smith, D. K. (2003). *The wisdom of teams: Creating the high performance organization*. New York, NY: Harper Collins.

Komives, S. R., Lucas, N., & McMahon, T. R. (2013). *Exploring leadership: For college students who want to make a difference* (3rd ed.). San Francisco, CA: Jossey-Bass.

Landreman, L. M. (Ed.). (2013). *The art of effective facilitation: Reflections from social justice educators*. Sterling, VA: Stylus.

Lencioni, P. (2002). *The five dysfunctions of a team: A leadership fable*. San Francisco, CA: Jossey-Bass.

Outcalt, C., Farris, S., & McMahon, K. (Eds.). (2000). *Developing non-hierarchical leadership on campus: Case studies and best practices in higher education*. Westport, CT: Greenwood.

Patterson, K., Grenny, J., McMillan, R., Switzler, A., & Roppé, L. (2013). *Crucial conversations: Tools for talking when stakes are high* (2nd ed.). Grand Haven, MI: Brilliance Audio.

Shankman, M. L., Allen, S. J., Haber-Curran, P. (2015). *Emotionally intelligent leadership: A guide for students* (2nd ed.). San Francisco, CA: Jossey-Bass.

Stone, D., Heen, S., & Patton, B. (2010). *Difficult conversations: How to discuss what matters most*. New York, NY: Penguin Books.

Zuniga, X., Nagda, B., Chesler, M., & Cytron-Walker, A. (2007). *Intergroup dialogue in higher education: Meaningful learning about social justice*. San Francisco, CA: Jossey-Bass.

› Media

Authenticity Consulting, LLC. Interpersonal listening skills: www.managementhelp.org/commskls/listen/listen.htm

The Intercultural Conflict Style Inventory: An Innovative Tool for Resolving Conflicts Across Cultural Boundaries: www.icsinventory.com/

Thandie Newton (2011 July). TED Talk: Embracing otherness, embracing myself. Retrieved from: www.ted.com/talks/thandie_newton_embracing_otherness_embracing_myself?language=en

Celeste Headlee (2015 May). TED Talk: 10 ways to have a better conversation. Retrieved from: www.ted.com/talks/celeste_headlee_10_ways_to_have_a_better_conversation#

More TED Talks on communication: www.ted.com/topics/communication

Kate Torgovnick May (2013, December 9). I am because of you: Further reading on ubuntu [Web log post]. Retrieved from: http://blog.ted.com/further-reading-on-ubuntu

Public Conversations Project: www.publicconversations.org/

This I Believe, Inc. (2016). This I believe essay-writing guidelines. *thisibelieve.org*. Retrieved from: http://thisibelieve.org/guidelines

› Professional Organizations

Association for Conflict Resolution: www.imis100us2.com/ACR/ACR/

Campus Compact: www.compact.org

Intercultural Development Research Institute: www.idrinstitute.org

Public Conversations Project: www.publicconversations.org/

› Other Resources

Barnga: A Simulation Game on Cultural Clashes: https://www.hodder.co.uk/books/detail.page?isbn=9781931930307

Star Power: www.stsintl.net/schools-and-charities/products/starpower/

StrengthsFinder: www.strengthsfinder.com/home.aspx

> Suggested Questions for Discussion or Assignments

- A key element of Controversy with Civility is that resolution of differences is not always an outcome. Given this, how does practicing Controversy with Civility still contribute to a group's process?

- Controversy with Civility encourages one to develop an awareness of others' world-views. What are ways in which individuals and groups can support and sustain this practice?

- What do you think may contribute to a person's approach to engaging with controversy online versus the way in which they might engage with controversy in person?

- At the heart of Controversy with Civility is the question of how you respond to difference—from difference of opinion or of beliefs, to differences of background or experience. How can we encounter difference in others with an eagerness to learn, rather than an aggressive or protective response?

- How do issues of power and privilege affect Controversy with Civility? How do systems of oppression and dominance affect what gets discussed, who gets to discuss, and how issues are framed in conversations?

- We often have a tendency to falsely believe that others' lives, motivations, experiences, and beliefs are not as complex as our own. Reflect on a time when you realized you were making this assumption about someone else. How can we best guard against these assumptions about others, and why is it important to do so?

- Perspective-taking is a critical skill for practicing Controversy with Civility well. How have you in the past been able to successfully step out of your own shoes and into some-one else's? What is the limitation in doing so, and how can we get better at it? Can we ever fully know what it's like in someone else's shoes?

- Data show that Controversy with Civility is typically the least developed of the eight C values amongst college students. Why do you think this is? How can colleges and universities better create opportunities for developing this C? What have been some of your most meaningful learning opportunities around this concept?

- What have been your experiences with controversy online? How have these experiences shaped your approach to engaging with controversy online and in person?

> References

This I Believe, Inc (2016). A public dialogue about belief - one essay at a time. *thisibelieve.org*. Retrieved August 04, 2016, from www.thisibelieve.org

Alvarez, C. (2017). Controversy with civility. In S. R. Komives, W. Wagner, & Associates (Eds.), *Leadership for a better world: Understanding the Social Change Model of Leadership Development* (2nd Ed.; pp. 149–170). San Francisco, CA: Jossey-Bass.

Arao, B., & Clemens, K. (2013). From safe spaces to brave spaces. In L. M. Landreman (Ed.), *The art of effective facilitation: Reflections from social justice educators* (pp. 135–150). Sterling, VA: Stylus.

Boyd, R. (2006). The value of civility? *Urban Studies, 43,* 863–878. doi: 10.1080/00420980600676105

Bucher, R. D. (2004). *Diversity Consciousness: Opening our minds to people, cultures, and opportunities* (2nd ed.). Upper Saddle River, NJ: Pearson Prentice Hall.

Dugan, J. P., Bohle, C. W., Woelker, L. R., & Cooney, M. A. (2014). The role of social perspective-taking in developing students' leadership capacities. *Journal of Student Affairs Research and Practice, 51*(1), 1–15. doi: 10.1515/jsarp-2014-0001

Dugan, J. P., Kodama, C., Correia, B., & Associates. (2013). *Multi-Institutional Study of Leadership insight report: Leadership program delivery.* College Park, MD: National Clearinghouse for Leadership Programs.

Dugan, J. P., & Komives, S. R. (2007). Developing leadership capacity in college students: Findings from a national study. *A report from the Multi-Institutional Study of Leadership.* College Park, MD: National Clearinghouse for Leadership Programs.

Galinsky, A. D., Ku, G., & Wang, C. S. (2005). Perspective-taking and self-other overlap: Fostering social bonds and facilitating social coordination. *Group Processes & Intergroup Relations, 8,* 109–124. doi: 10.1177/1368430205051060

How do questions advance dialogue? (n.d.). Watertown, MA: Public Conversations Project. Retrieved from: www.publicconversations.org/sites/default/files/sec10.pdf

Public Conversations Project. (n.d). Retrieved August 04, 2016, from www.publicconversations.org

Rian Satterwhite serves as director of the Holden Center for Leadership and Community Engagement at the University of Oregon. Rian has served as Chair of the Leadership Education member interest group in the International Leadership Association, and has published on the topics of sustainability leadership, systems perspectives, and future leadership. He attended the University of Arizona for his bachelor's degree in Interdisciplinary Studies, and the University of Wollongong (Australia) for his Masters of Educational Leadership, earned with distinction.

Christopher Ruiz de Esparza serves as associate director of the Holden Center for Leadership and Community Engagement at the University of Oregon. Chris grounds his work in experience with leadership development, group facilitation, improvisation, diversity and inclusion, and applied psychology. He attended Stanford University for his bachelor's degree in psychology, and the University of California-Santa Barbara for his master's and doctoral work in counseling psychology.

Chapter 11

Citizenship

Benjamin P. Correia-Harker

> Summary of Key Concepts

Citizenship is the sole value within the Society/Community level of the Social Change Model (SCM) of Leadership Development. More than just membership in a community, Citizenship is both a mindset that recognizes the interconnected nature of the individual with other community members and active engagement with others to better the community, including forming coalitions among groups in a community (Bonnet, 2017). The word citizenship might be uncomfortable for campuses engaging undocumented students, international students, or those who think of citizenship as a governmental concept of voting; however, this concept is intended to be interpreted broadly, with a focus on community and stewardship.

Community consists of two components: 1) a group of people with shared interests, perspectives, attitudes, and goals; and 2) engagement in a collective responsibility to achieve something greater than oneself (Bonnet, 2017). Some argue that everyone has the capacity to practice engaged citizenship anywhere in their communities. Community engagement can take many forms, from socially responsible personal behavior, to direct service, to political involvement.

When attending to Citizenship, understanding several concepts will provide individuals with greater capacity for engagement. One such concept is *social capital*, which refers to power accumulated from "networks, norms, and social trust that facilitate coordinated and cooperative for mutual benefit" (Putnam, 1999, p. 573). A second key concept is that of *empowerment*, or recognizing which members feel empowered, and therefore motivated and able to influence change, as opposed to members who feel disenfranchised and, thus, constrained from fully engaging in the community. *Social perspective-taking* is another important concept, highlighting the value of one's ability to understand how others think or feel (Dugan et al., 2014). Lastly, individuals must know how *coalitions*, or collections of groups that maintain distinctive identities yet work together for a common cause, are necessary to address society's complex social problems.

More recently, Citizenship has taken form through digital citizenship and consumer activism. Social media is becoming a prominent medium for community engagement; yet the value of this form of hashtag activism and social movements formed through social media is often debated, with some arguing that it is too passive, and others recognizing its potential to galvanize greater action. Whereas many are familiar with boycotting as a form of consumer activism, "buycotting" is a newer adaptation where individuals purchase goods or services to endorse beliefs or actions of particular companies.

> Supportive Research Findings

Several studies pinpoint critical factors and concepts that help individuals better understand and develop the capacity to enact Citizenship. Dugan and Komives (2011) explored a number of demographic and environmental variables related to the Citizenship value and identified a few key factors facilitators may leverage, such as:

- Participation in community service
- Socio-cultural conversations with peers (that is, conversations about and across difference)

- Mentoring relationships
- Fostering leadership self-efficacy, that is, participants' belief in their ability to be successful at leadership (Bandura, 1997)

Facilitators may want to integrate these practices into participant experiences in order to effectively promote leadership development, particularly as it relates to the Citizenship value.

Recently, Johnson (2015) confirmed that a meaningful relationship exists between social change behaviors (for example, signing a petition, taking part in a demonstration, or being active in an organization to address social issues) and Citizenship. Providing opportunities for participants to engage in social change experiences can be a powerful opportunity to help them develop a stronger civic identity and capacity for Citizenship.

It is also important to acknowledge certain populations who tend to report lower or higher scores on this value of the Social Change Model. African American and Black students report significantly higher scores on Citizenship, whereas Asian and Asian American students report significantly lower scores (Dugan, Komives, & Segar, 2009). The value of Citizenship may resonate with African American and Black participants due to strong historical and cultural traditions for this community drawn from civil rights activism. Thus, this may be a strong entry point for African American and Black participants trying to understand their way of being in the leadership process. Tailoring experiences based on the participants is critical to maximize an intervention's impact. Capitalizing on knowledge gleaned from research will help leadership educators to better leverage diverse participant learning related to the value of Citizenship.

› Activities Overview

The activities in this chapter provide facilitators with experiences that capitalize on diverse ways of knowing and learning to help participants explore central Citizenship concepts. Activity One, *Images of Citizenship and Community*, challenges participants to make their own and collective meanings of citizenship and community using photography as a central tool. In the second activity, *Expanding Levels of Community*, participants will recognize different levels of community in which they are involved and critically reflect on their role in those communities. Participants learn about different ways of being and engaging in communities through Activity Three, *Citizenship for Social Change Panel*. Scenarios that challenge participants to explore different lenses of complex situations are at the heart of the Activity Four, *Social-Perspective-Taking through Case Studies*. Activity Five, *Community Decision-Making: In the Room Where It Happens*, helps participants explore power, who has access to decision-making, and what motivates them to engage in communities.

Estimated Time

Activity One: *Images of Citizenship and Community*, 40 minutes

Activity Two: *Expanding Levels of Community*, 30 minutes

Activity Three: *Citizenship for Social Change Panel*, 50 to 60 minutes

Activity Four: *Social Perspective-Taking through Case Studies*, 60 minutes

Activity Five: *Community Decision-Making: In the Room Where It Happens*, 20 minutes

> Learning Activities

Activity One: Images of Citizenship and Community

Time: 40 minutes

Learning Outcomes   Participants will

- Develop a clearer understanding of citizenship and community.
- Recognize and consider different interpretations of citizenship and community.

Materials

- Camera and/or camera phone (*Note*: Some participants may not have access to this resource, so you may need to identify other ways participants can access a camera.)
- Notecards

Detailed Instructions   Prior to meeting, instruct participants to take pictures of anything they believe represents their understandings of Citizenship and community. Ask them to take 2 or 3 pictures that represent each concept to share with the group. For each picture, participants should note a few reasons why each particular image represents their understanding of Citizenship and community. Ask participants to print copies of the pictures to bring with them.

When meeting, divide participants into groups of 3 or 4 members to discuss their pictures and conceptions of Citizenship and community for 20 minutes. In the small groups, have each participant present their pictures and discuss their understandings of the concepts. After everyone has shared, ask them to consider these questions:

- Where do they see overlap between the ways that all of them understood these two concepts?
- Where do they see disagreement between what each concept means?

Bring the small groups back to the whole group and engage in a larger conversation about common threads for their understanding of Citizenship and community for 20 minutes. Some common themes for discussion:

- Have each group report out commonalities with their definitions. What consistent commonalities exist across all groups?
- What are divergent perspectives? Why might some connotations of citizenships and community be different?
- If participants were assigned readings about Citizenship and community, how are their understandings consistent and/or divergent with the readings?

By the end of the session, the group should come to a collective understanding of citizenship and community for future conversations/projects while recognizing that these concepts have nuanced meanings for different individuals and groups.

Pass out the notecards, and for 5 minutes, have participants use each side of the notecard to answer each of these questions:

- How did this experience confirm or solidify their understanding of community or citizenship?
- How did this experience challenge their original perceptions of community or citizenship?

Facilitator Notes   If the group is a smaller one, consider breaking into smaller groups and instead have each individual present their pictures to the entire group. Participants could also take the pictures on phones and bring them to share on the phones instead of printing the pictures; but keep in mind that not all participants may have access to this technology.

Activity Two: Expanding Levels of Community

Time: 30 minutes

Learning Outcomes   Participants will

- Identify various levels of communities to which they belong.
- Consider the interconnected nature of multiple communities.
- Integrate understandings of different forms of Citizenship with different communities.

Materials
- Poster paper
- Markers

Detailed Instructions Distribute paper and markers to participants and ask them to draw a small circle on their paper. In that small circle, ask them to identify a community to which they belong (for instance, a choir, intramural team, residence hall floor, sorority, political group, church, etc.). (*5 minutes*)

For that community, ask them to make notes for 5 minutes, and respond to the following questions:

- What are the shared interests of individuals in this community?
- What is the greater aim of this community? What is this community trying to achieve?
- What are the ways that you participate in this community? (Participants may refer to Exhibit 9.1: "Forms of Individual Civic Engagement" in *Leadership for a Better World*, 2017.)

Next, have participants draw a larger circle around the smaller circle and identify a larger community in which their original community is nested. For example, if a participant identifies an interfaith club as their smaller community, examples of larger communities in which the original community is nested could be the larger organization for which the club is a chapter, the religious/spiritual community on campus, the network of clubs at school, the interfaith community in the town/city, or even the general interfaith movement. Another example may be a fraternity or sorority as the smaller circle. Thus, a larger circle encompassing the smaller one may be fraternity and sorority life in general at the institution, the national chapter of the fraternity or sorority, male/masculinity and women's groups, or a philanthropic entity with which the fraternity or sorority chapter is connected. The goal is to expand the participants' understanding of community beyond immediate groups in which they are involved to include larger communities in which they may not realize they are a member. (*5 minutes*)

For this larger community, ask the participants the same set of questions:

- What are the shared interests of individuals in this community?
- What is the greater aim of this community? What is this community trying to achieve?
- What are the ways that you participate in this community?

Once they answer the questions above, ask the participants to reflect on how their answers are the different or the same, and why that may be.

Once participants have reflected on these two layers of community, have them pair up and discuss the communities and responses to questions. Ask the pairs to spent 10 minutes discussing how their conception of their role and participation in each layer of community shifts, using the following questions:

- Do participants even recognize themselves as part of the larger community?
- What sense of responsibility do participants have toward these larger communities?

For 5 minutes, have participants report back their collective wisdom to the larger group. Collective wisdom is *not* reporting out everything discussed in the partner conversation. Instead, collective wisdom is sharing any particular insights individuals had that they believe would benefit the larger group.

Facilitator Notes   Be prepared to provide examples for the second stage of this activity. Participants may struggle to understand what is meant by identifying a larger community in which the original one is nested.

Activity Three: Citizenship for Social Change Panel

Time: 60 minutes

Learning Outcomes   Participants will

- Understand different ways of engaging as a citizen to promote social change.
- Recognize the importance of history and context for community change.

- Apply different ways of engaging with their own identity and participation in communities.

Detailed Instructions

Preparation: Select a panel of 3 to 5 individuals who are active in diverse communities and engaged in social change in those areas in different ways. When considering panelists, choose individuals who:

- Do this work for a living and those who volunteer
- Have a formal leadership role and those who do not
- Represent a diverse range of social change issues and scales of communities
- Come with different vantage points within their communities

Provide panelists with preparation instructions and questions to consider for the group, such as the following:

- Tell us a little bit about yourself and why you're involved with this community. What prompted you to become an engaged citizen?
- Tell us about the community. Who composes this community, what is the community's history, and what is the community's purpose?
- How do you see yourself as an engaged citizen in this community?
- How have you been able to help your community advance its aims?
- What are some important lessons you learned about effectively engaging in this community?
- What did you learn about the community in this process? About yourself?
- What advice would you give to others seeking to be more engaged citizens?

Provide participants with a basic overview of the panel's purpose, and ask them to prepare at least one question to ask the panelists about their work in their communities.

Activity Implementation:

- Introduce the panelists (and if the group is small enough, have participants introduce themselves as well). (*5 minutes*)

- Allow panelists time to tell the stories of who they are and how they are engaged as active citizens in their respective communities. (*20 minutes*)
- Open up the panel for participants to ask questions. As a facilitator, you may want to have a couple questions prepared to start the conversation. (*20 minutes*)
- Allow panelists to provide closing thoughts. (*5 minutes*)

Reflection: Once the panel is completed, provide space for participants to reflect on the following questions for 10 minutes. Depending on the group, these can be individual reflection questions, or addressed through conversations in pairs:

- What aspects of the panelist conversations resonated with you? What aspects challenged your way of thinking about Citizenship in a community?
- What did you notice about panelists' mindsets for engaging their community? How might this understanding influence ways that you'll think about your Citizenship in various communities?
- What did you notice about panelists' diverse forms of engagement with their communities? How does this inform how you should be active in different communities to which you belong?

Facilitator Notes   If you are working with a group dedicated to a specific topic or population, consider finding panelists related to that topic (for instance, panelists working in environmentalism for a sustainability-focused group). Or, consider finding other students who are engaged in the work of social change to provide a peer perspective. This activity is similar in delivery to the third activity, *Commitment Panel*, in Chapter Seven, "Commitment," and both activities may be combined if desired.

Activity Four: Social Perspective-Taking through Case Studies[1]

Time: 60 minutes

Learning Outcomes   Participants will

- Analyze complex community issues that affect a community, by understanding the lenses of different stakeholders and recognizing different forms of power.
- Apply leadership concepts from other SCM values to complex social scenarios.
- Care for the health of a community when engaging with divisive issues in a community.

Materials

- Interfaith Youth Core's "Case Studies for Exploring Interfaith Cooperation: Classroom Tools," which are available online at www.ifyc.org/resources/case-studies-exploring-interfaith-cooperation-classroom-tools/.

Detailed Instructions   Case studies are powerful tools to help participants apply concepts to real (or realistic) situations and can be complicated with multifaceted issues and a range of stakeholders. The Interfaith Youth Core (www.ifyc.com) has collected a number of case studies that help individuals explore some of these complex issues. Select 1 of the 4 case studies that you believe will engage the group of participants.

Provide participants with Part 1 of the selected case study to read silently (or have participants read portions aloud). (*5 to 10 minutes*)

Divide participants into smaller groups of 3 to 5 individuals. Use the questions provided in the case study document to guide the conversation, but also consider these additional questions. Make sure participants spend time

[1] Adapted from and used with permission of Suomala, K. R., & Interfaith Youth Core. (2013). Case studies for exploring interfaith cooperation: Classroom tools. Retrieved from: www.ifyc.org/resources/case-studies-exploring-interfaith-cooperation-classroom-tools/.

exploring the different components of the case study. Often, participants will want to jump into articulating a solution, so encourage them to take this time to discuss the questions and different perspectives on the situation. (*20 minutes*)

Additional questions to consider:

- What different communities are involved in these scenarios?
- What is at jeopardy for the well-being of the respective communities?
- How are different stakeholders engaging or disengaging?

Once groups have discussed key factors in the case, ask them to come up with a recommended course of action. This course of action may be from an omniscient or omnipotent perspective, and transcending particular roles or suggesting ideal courses of action. Or participants can give a recommended course of action for a particular stakeholder in the situation. (*10 minutes*)

Have each group present their recommendation to the larger group, explaining why they believe this course of action is best for the communities involved. (*10 minutes*)

Provide participants with Part 2 of the case study and allow them time to read silently (or in some sort of group reading process). (*5 minutes*)

In a large group discussion, ask participants to share their opinions of how the situation was handled. (*10 minutes*)

Additional questions for discussion:

- How does the Part 2 align with their proposals?
- What do they appreciate about how the situation was handled? What do they think should have been handled differently?

After discussing Part 2, if time allows, challenge participants to imagine themselves as a member of the broader community in the scenario. They are not in any specific role directly related to the case at hand, but, nonetheless, are part of that community. If they became aware of this situation, how would they engage? Would they honestly even engage with this situation?

Facilitator Notes   The background and case studies provided in Chapter Three, "Using Case Studies," provide additional information on using case studies. The case studies from Chapter Three may also be used with this activity.

Activity Five: Community Decision-Making: In the Room Where It Happens

Time: 25 minutes

Learning Outcomes   Participants will

- Recognize power differentials exist related to who has access to decision-making in communities (social capital).
- Critique/analyze how decision-making happens within larger communities, particularly the government.
- Reflect upon personal motivations for civic engagement and leadership.

Materials
- The song, "The Room Where It Happens," from the Broadway musical, *Hamilton*. (*5:18 minutes*) (*Note*: The individual song can be purchased through various digital media sources such as iTunes, Amazon, or Google Play. It is also possible to find the song available with memberships to streaming services such as Spotify, Amazon Prime, or Apple Music, but this is not guaranteed.)
- A handout or visual display of the song lyrics. Lyrics can be found at the soundtrack website (http://atlanticrecords.com/HamiltonMusic/), or by searching online for the lyrics.

Detailed Instructions   For this activity, choose a historical case, a current story on a social issue, a fictional text novel, a movie, documentary, or television series, or a song to illustrate how communities come together to make decisions. Pick a scenario in which students can see how power plays a role in who has access to conversations about decisions; who has power when advocating for particular ends, and what kind of power they have; and what motivates different people to engage in the process.

To illustrate this activity, a song from *Hamilton*, the Broadway musical, will be used.

Introduce the activity to participants by letting them know you are going to listen to a song and reflect on its message, and make meaning of this in relation to Citizenship. Prior to the song, ask them to consider a the following questions while listening to the song:

- What key points is the song trying to make?
- What are the main motivations of the characters in the song? (The characters include Thomas Jefferson, James Madison, Alexander Hamilton, and Aaron Burr.)

Play the song for participants, and have them read along with the lyrics. (*Song Duration: 5:18*)

Engage participants in a group conversation about the song. First, explore the key points of the song. Facilitators may want to give participants time to reflect on this individually before discussing with the group, using the following questions. (*15 minutes*)

Discussion Questions

- What do participants believe the key points are?
- Did people interpret key points differently? How so, and why?
- How do these key points overlap with core concepts of Citizenship? Social capital? Empowerment and marginalization in communities?
- What are the motivations for each character?
- What do participants think of each person's source of motivation?
- What motivates participants to engage in various communities?

Facilitator Notes   Use judgment as to whether to provide some context for the song. The song should be able to be understood on its own with a basic understanding of U.S. history. In other countries, there may be other musical selections about political movements that are more appropriate (for instance, *Les Miserables* in France).

Encourage participants to critically interrogate their motivations for involvement in different communities. Participants may espouse altruistic aims as their motivation, but challenge them to dig a level deeper, assessing where those altruistic intentions come from:

- They want to be seen as a good person.
- They want to make a mark and/or leave a legacy.
- They believe they can make the community better.
- There are particular individuals in the community about whom they care deeply.

› Supplemental Readings

Alquist, J., & Endersby, L. (2017). *New Directions for Student Leadership: No. 153. Going digital in student leadership*. San Francisco, CA: Jossey-Bass.

Barberá, P., Wang, N., Bonneau, R., Jost, J. T., Nagler, J., Tucker, J., & González-Bailón, S. (2015). The critical periphery in the growth of social protests. *PloS one, 10*(11), e0143611. doi: 10.1371/journal.pone.0143611. Also available at http://journals.plos.org/plosone/article?id=10.1371/journal.pone.0143611

Bordas, J. (2012). *Salsa, soul, and spirit: Leadership for a multicultural age*. San Francisco, CA: Berrett-Koehler Publishers.

Chod, S., Muck, W., & Caliendo, S. (2015). *Technology and civic engagement in the college classroom engaging the unengaged*. New York, NY: Palgrave Macmillan.

Colby, A., Ehrlich, T., Beaumont, E., & Stephens, J. (2003). *Educating citizens: Preparing America's undergraduates for lives of moral and civic responsibility*. San Francisco, CA: Jossey-Bass.

Dewey, J. (1944). *Democracy and education*. New York, NY: The Free Press.

Green, D. (2012). *From Poverty to Power: How active citizens and effective states can change the world* (2nd ed). Rugby, UK: Practical Action Publishing and Oxford: Oxfam International. Available for download at www.oxfamamerica.org/static/media/files/From_Poverty_to_Power_2nd_Edition.pdf.

Jacoby, B. (2015). *Service-learning essentials: Questions, answers, and lessons learned*. San Francisco, CA: Jossey-Bass.

Jacoby, B., & Associates. (2009). *Civic engagement in higher education: Concepts and practices.* San Francisco, CA: Jossey-Bass.

Loeb, P. (2010). *Soul of a citizen: Living with conviction in challenging times.* New York, NY: St. Martin's Griffin.

Moore, T. L. (2014). *Community-University engagement: A process for building democratic communities.* ASHE Higher Education Report, 40(2). San Francisco, CA: Jossey-Bass.

Munoz, L., & Spruck Wrigley, H. (Eds.). (2012). *Adult civic engagement in adult learning: New directions for adult and continuing education, No. 135.* Hoboken, NJ: John Wiley & Sons, Inc.

Patel, E. (2012). *Sacred ground: Pluralism, prejudice, and the promise of America.* Boston, MA: Beacon Press.

Preskill, S., & Brookfield, S. D. (2009). *Learning as a way of leading: Lessons from the struggle for social justice.* San Francisco, CA: Jossey-Bass.

Sinek, S. (2009). *Start with why: How great leaders inspire everyone to take action.* New York, NY: Portfolio.

Wagner, W., & Pigza, J. (Eds.). (2016). *New Directions for Student Leadership: No. 150. Leadership development through service-learning.* San Francisco, CA: Jossey-Bass.

› Media

The Atlantic Magazine: www.theatlantic.com/

Vox: www.vox.com

The American Conservative: www.theamericanconservative.com

The National Review: www.nationalreview.com

David Miller (2011, November 14). TEDx Talk:Redefining citizenship. Retrieved from: www.youtube.com/watch?v=STsOdmkH5fI

Simran Sethi (2012, July 12). TEDx Talk: Why and how do we engage? Retrieved from: www.youtube.com/watch?v=dk2nNhbocII

Ben Warner (2013, December 10). TEDx Talk: New models of civic engagement. Retrieved from: www.youtube.com/watch?v=NpCzIniPZDU

Shakuntala Banaji (2014, July 17). TED Talk: Young people, the internet and civic participation. Retrieved from: www.youtube.com/watch?v=ejtdq58dBW4

Lina Loved (2014, April 4). *Heartwarming Thai Commercial – Thai Good Stories by Linaloved* [Video file]. Retrieved from: www.youtube.com/watch?v=cZGghmwUcbQ

Common Knowledge podcast: www.ifyc.org/podcast

Global Development podcast from The Guardian: www.theguardian.com/global-development/series/global-development-podcast

Professional Organizations

American Democracy Project: www.aascu.org/programs/ADP

Association of American Colleges & Universities, Civic Learning and Democratic Engagement: www.aacu.org/clde

Campus Compact: http://compact.org

Center for Information & Research on Civic Learning and Engagement (CIRCLE): http://civicyouth.org

Do Something: www.dosomething.org/us

Interfaith Youth Core: www.ifyc.org

Suggested Questions for Discussions or Assignments

- In which communities do you consider yourself a part? What does Citizenship in those communities mean to you? How are you actively involved in these communities?
- The term Citizenship has different meanings to different people. How do you define it?
- What do you believe are the indicators of "good" Citizenship?
- What does it mean to be actively or passively engaged in your communities?
- What forms of Citizenship and community involvement appeal to you most? What does it mean that you prefer certain forms of civic engagement over others?
- Do certain forms of civic engagement perpetuate or create issues in some communities?
- Within the communities of which you're a part, how do you develop social capital and increase your awareness of issues in those communities?
- Who feels empowered to engage in the community and who may feel excluded? Who is listened to? Who determines who is listened to?
- Is your social capital stronger or weaker in different pockets of the community? Why is that so?
- What issues exist in your community? Does everyone perceive these issues in the same way?

> References

Bandura, A. (1997). *Self-efficacy: The exercise of control.* New York, NY: W. H. Freeman.

Bonnet, J. (2017). Citizenship. In S. R. Komives, W. Wagner, & Associates, *Leadership for a better world* (*2nd ed.; pp. 175–198*). San Francisco, CA: Jossey-Bass.

Dugan, J. P. & Komives, S. R. (2011). Influences on college students' capacity for socially responsible leadership. *Journal of College Student Development, 51,* 525–549. doi: 10.1353/csd.2010.0009

Dugan, J. P., Komives, S. R., & Segar, T. C. (2009). College student capacity for socially responsible leadership: Understanding norms and influences of race, gender, and sexual orientation. *NASPA Journal, 45,* 475-500. doi: 10.2202/1949-6605.2008

Dugan, J. P., Bohle, C. W., Woelker, L. R., & Cooney, M. A. (2014). The role of social perspective-taking in developing students' leadership capacities. *Journal of Student Affairs Research and Practice, 51,* 1–15. doi: 10.1515/jsarp-2014-0001

Johnson, M. (2015). Developing college students' civic identity: The role of social perspective taking and sociocultural issues discussions. *Journal of College Student Development, 56,* 687–704. doi: 10.1353/csd.2015.0074

Putnam, R. D. (1999). Bowling alone: America's declining social capital. In B. Barber & R. M. Battistoni (Eds.), *Education for democracy* (pp. 553– 557). Dubuque, IA: Kendall/Hunt.

Suomala, K. R., & Interfaith Youth Core. (2013). *Case studies for exploring interfaith cooperation: Classroom tools.* Retrieved from www.ifyc.org/resources/case-studies-exploring-interfaith-cooperation-classroom-tools/.

Benjamin P. Correia-Harker is Director of Campus Assessment at the Interfaith Youth Core, a non-profit organization that partners with higher education to promote interfaith cooperation toward civic good. He has a Ph.D. in Higher Education from Loyola University Chicago, and his research focuses on the role motivation plays in leadership development.

Chapter 12

Change

Melissa L. Rocco

> Summary of the Key Concepts

This chapter examines the concept of Change within the Social Change Model (SCM) of Leadership Development, as well as processes and considerations for making change in individuals, groups, and society/community. There are two major types of change. *Single-order change* involves structural or procedural changes within the present state of an organization. *Second-order*, or *transformative change*, involves changing values, assumptions, and ultimately the culture of an organization (Boyce, 2003; Eckel, Hill, & Green, 1998). Transformative change can be described as an organic process: it occurs in systems not compartments; is constant not episodic; is exponential not linear; and it can be influenced but not controlled (Wagner, 2017).

Scholars have identified two types of challenges facing individuals, groups, and communities: technical challenges and adaptive challenges (Heifetz, Grashow &; Linsky, 2009; Heifetz &; Laurie, 1997; Heifetz & Linksy, 2002). *Technical challenges* can be addressed through existing solutions, whereas *adaptive challenges* require a new way of thinking to make change. Understanding our own mental models (Senge, 2006; 2014), and the lens through which we view the world, helps to identify our approach to technical challenges. Kegan and Lahey's (2009) research helps illuminate the ways in which shifting our mental models helps with Individual level change and addressing adaptive challenges. This approach to understanding challenges and change also applies to Group and Society/Community level change.

When engaging in any change-making effort at this level, it is helpful to remember that communities/societies are more like networked systems that are nonlinear and can be influenced, but not fully controlled. In general, people take one of three approaches to change: they make it, survive it, or let it happen organically. Allen and Cherrey (2000) suggest four metaphors for understanding how organic change happens: wet sand (through the use of force and resistance); birds on a wire (as individuals test different options and gradually gather support from others to move forward); yeast (certain individuals serve as the catalysts for change under the right conditions); and the beneficial virus (when influence and resistance spread rapidly through the network).

Finally, it is important to understand why and how people resist change (Bridges, 2003; Kegan & Lahey, 2009). Resistance happens both actively and passively. For example, while some may be overly critical or try to sabotage change efforts, others may say they agree with the change but just not follow-through. When leaders encounter resistance to change, they should reflect on the characteristics of networked systems and organic change to help guide their actions. Rather than imposing rules and punishments to force change, leaders should think of change-making as facilitating a process of learning and development for all involved.

› Activities Overview

Activity One, *Primer: Change Quotes*, serves as a primer to get participants thinking about the various components and complexities of change. Participants select quotes that resonate with them about change and share insights in reflective discussion. The second activity, *Individual Change: "This is Water,"* is an engaging video about the importance of self-awareness and examining our assumptions and mindsets in order make personal change. Activity Three, *Group Change: A View from the Balcony*, asks participants to conduct an organizational analysis and determine what is helping or hindering a specific group or team to engage in change. Finally, Activity Four, *Society/Community Change: What's Holding the World Back?*, gives participants the chance to find an educational video about a social issue of their choice and reflect on the complexities of making widespread change in society.

Estimated Time

Activity One: *Primer: Change Quotes*, 3 minutes per participant, 5 to 10 minutes group discussion

Activity Two: *Individual Change: "This Is Water,"* 60 to 75 minutes

Activity Three: *Group Change: A View from the Balcony*, 90 to 120 minutes

Activity Four: *Society/Community Change: What's Holding the World Back?*, 90 to 120 minutes preparation, 30 to 45 minutes in-person activity and reflective discussion

> Learning Activities

Activity One: Primer: Change Quotes

Time: 5 to 10 minute reflective discussion (3 minutes per participant)

Learning Outcomes   Participants will

- Consider the nature of change and what is required of individuals to understand, embrace, and manage change in themselves, their groups, and their communities.
- Understand others' perspectives on important elements of a change process.

- Develop verbal communication skills by sharing quotes and thoughts that resonate with their understanding of change.

Materials
- Computer (optional)
- Projector and screen (optional)
- Audio/Visual connection (optional)

Detailed Instructions   Before the session, ask participants to search the internet, books, magazines, and other publications to find quotes about change. Each participant should choose a quote that resonates with them to share with the group. For example: a participant may believe that change requires being open to learning new things and listening to new perspectives. The quote they choose could be: "In times of change the learner will inherit the Earth, while the learned will find themselves well equipped to deal with a world that no longer exists," by Eric Hoffer.

Once participants have identified a quote to share, ask them to create a visual aid that includes the quote as well as pictures, drawings, and designs that help express the meaning of the quote.

You may choose to have participants do this via visual presentation software and use a projector and screen to display their presentation for the class. Alternatively, this could be an art project where you ask participants to use paper, markers, crayons, and other creative arts materials.

Participants should bring their completed quote visual to the educational session to share with other participants. Give each participant approximately 3 minutes to share their quote, why they chose it, and to describe their visual.

After each participant has had a chance to share, engage the large group in a reflective discussion about common themes across the quotes that were shared. If time allows, ask participants to share personal examples of when they have dealt with a particular change theme. Finally, ask the group to reflect on why they believe these themes are important to keep in mind as you move forward with the session.

Facilitator Notes This activity serves as a primer for the rest of the activities discussing change, change management, and resistance to change. Make note of the themes found in the quotes that participants share and bring those back into the conversation later.

A variation on this activity would be to provide the participants with time during the activity to find quotes and create their visual aid. The facilitator may also decide to provide quote books and other resources as appropriate, or may decide to bring in a collection of quotes about change that represent a variety of viewpoints, and have participants choose a quote that they would like to share from this collection.

Activity Two: Individual Change: "This Is Water"

Time: 60 to 70 minutes

Learning Outcomes Participants will

- Reflect on their assumptions about human nature, groups of people, and how the world works.
- Understand the importance of self-awareness for self-transformation, and how examining and renegotiating our assumptions serves as the foundation for individual change.

Materials
- Computer and internet access for video streaming
- Projector and screen
- Speakers
- Audio/Visual connection
- Sticky notes or small slips of paper (Approximately 10 per participant)
- Writing utensils

Detailed Instructions Inform participants that they will watch a video about self-awareness, self-transformation, and the choices we make about how we see and interact with the world. The video illustrates part of a speech given by David Foster Wallace at Kenyon College in 2005.

"This Is Water" is available as a video or a transcript. Many versions exist and can be easily found by searching on the internet. It is also available in book format; see *This Is Water: Some Thoughts, Delivered on a Significant Occasion, about Living a Compassionate Life* by David Foster Wallace (2009).

Engage participants in a reflective discussion about the video/speech:

- What are your initial reactions to this message?
- What are the main messages found in this speech?
- What parts of the message resonate with you?
- What does this speech have to do with self-awareness? Self-transformation?
- How does personal perception, frames, mindset, and mental models—our "natural default setting"—affect our ability to change as individuals?
- Can you think of any personal examples where you have resorted to your "natural default setting" and not made conscious choices about how you think, feel, and behave?

If participants do not make these connections in the reflective discussion on their own, point out the importance of recognizing our own default setting—our assumptions and perceptions, which can function like the air we breathe, or like water to a fish—before we are able to go through self-transformation.

Explain that the group will now spend time identifying their own "natural default settings." Have participants write on sticky notes or slips of paper some of their assumptions and perceptions about various things (for instance, groups of people, places, human nature, the way the world works, or things they take for granted). These responses can remain anonymous, or you can ask participants to identify themselves; do whatever is most appropriate for the particular participant group.

Place all of the written responses in a central location in the room, and have the participants organize the responses into themes. Have the participants make a master list of the themes that can be posted or projected in the room for all to see.

Divide the participants into small groups of 3 to 5 individuals and have them discuss what they believe it will take for them to change their assumptions, perceptions, and mindsets about the themes listed in the previous step. (*Optional*: Participants may also find Kegan and Lahey's [2009] research on individual level change and the importance of adapting mental models and Dweck's [2006] concept of growth mindset as helpful references for this discussion. This information can be provided by the facilitator or assigned for personal research and reading prior to the session.)

Gather the large group back together to share highlights from their small group conversations. Make any final summary points regarding the topics of self-awareness, self-transformation, and action steps for individual change.

Facilitator Notes　　This activity can also be adapted into an online reflection or blog post prior to the class meeting, or for homework. Participants could watch or read the speech on their own, and write a personal reflection using the questions outlined above for small and large group discussions. The small and large group conversations could also be facilitated online through blogging websites or online learning management systems. This activity could also be modified to help groups and communities identify their collective mental models and action steps for addressing adaptive challenges.

Activity Three: Group Change: A View from the Balcony

Time: 90 to 120 minutes

Learning Outcomes　　Participants will

- Learn how to conduct an organizational analysis.
- Understand what helps and hinders a group in working toward major change.
- Practice creating action steps toward group change.

Materials
- Paper
- Writing utensils

Detailed Instructions   Explain to participants the concept of "getting on the balcony" (Heifetz & Linsky, 2002), which is a metaphor for examining a group of people from the outside looking in, and taking note of the way they interact and how they get work done. In essence, getting on the balcony helps us gain perspective we are often not able to see when we are in the middle of the group's everyday interactions.

Explain to participants that they will be conducting an organizational analysis of an organization or team in which they hold membership. Participants should each identify an organization or team and its stated purpose and mission, and record this information on a piece of paper or electronic device such as a laptop computer or tablet.

Divide the participants in small groups and ask them to share the following:

- The name of their chosen organization/team
- The stated mission/purpose of the organization/team
- Whether or not they believe the organization/team is succeeding in carrying out its mission/purpose. Why or why not? Provide an explanation and examples.

Have each participant engage in reflective writing with the following prompts. This can be done during the activity, or on their own outside of the session. For a more robust analysis, have participants meet with other members of the organization to discuss the prompts below before completing their written reflection:

- What elements of group dynamics help this organization/team to carry out its mission/purpose? What elements of group dynamics keep them from carrying out their mission/purpose? Think about organizational culture, group member expectations of each other, personal motivations, etc.
- What is the organization/team's "ideal state" compared to their reality? What do they want to do?
- What role do individual members play in helping or hindering the group's success?

- Why might the organization/team be struggling to change? Hultman (1998) and Wagner (2017) provide resources for assisting with frameworks related to understanding resistance.

In pairs, have the participants share a summary of their analysis. Have the pairs consider the assumptions of the organization and how that group mental model could be shifted to address adaptive challenges as an organization or team.

Bring the large group back together and ask for reflections, thoughts, and insights from their partner conversations. Make the point that change processes are complex and require deep understanding of an organization/team in order to craft a plan that will work and sustain the change.

Facilitator Notes   This activity could be modified in a variety of ways depending on the participant group, number of educational sessions, and desired depth of the learning experience. For example, the organizational analysis could be done individually or in small groups. The full activity could be done in a single educational session or as a long-term project across multiple sessions, including outside work. This activity could also be used as a long-term consulting project in which the participants work with an organization/team consistently over many weeks; or, it could just be a one-time research project.

Activity Four: Society/Community Change: What's Holding the World Back?

Time: 90 to 120 minutes preparation, 30 to 45 minute in-person activity and discussion

Learning Outcomes   Participants will

- Examine the complexity of large-scale social issues.
- Analyze the change-making process at a societal level.
- Understand the importance of creating and sustaining shared visions in order to make widespread societal change.

Materials
- Computer and internet access for video streaming
- Projector and screen
- Speakers
- Audio/Visual connection

Detailed Instructions   Prior to arriving at the educational session, participants should find and watch an online video of an educational talk on a major change initiative or social issue that has far-reaching impact.

Ask the participants to post the video to an online blog or discussion board that can be shared with the rest of the participants. Each participant should include in their post a written reflection on the following prompt:

- Consider a systems view of organizations to explain why you believe this social issue exists, and why it is so difficult to change. What do you think it will take to make major, lasting change related to this particular social issue? Allen and Cherrey (2000) and Kegan and Lahey (2009) are useful frameworks for considering this approach to organizations.

(*Optional*: Once participants arrive at the educational session in-person, ask participants to show their chosen videos and summarize their written reflection for the large group.)

Engage the group in a reflective conversation about the videos they chose, the related social issue, why these issues are so difficult to change, and what it will take to start making a difference. If each participant did not have time to share their video and reflection already, then ask for a few participants to share a verbal summary to get this conversation going in the large group.

Ask the group to reflect silently for a few moments on the following question: *What is a shared vision and why is it important for making lasting societal change?* Allow the participants to discuss amongst themselves, then share their insights with the larger group.

The point to make here is that a shared vision is not just what one person wants, but what people together decide is important and worth working toward. Shared visions are important in attempting to make societal change, because change efforts of that magnitude are complex and challenging, and require the investment of entire communities and populations. People need to feel personally connected to the vision, and that their voices are being heard and considered, in order to truly commit to the change effort.

Facilitator Notes   If time is a concern, divide the participants into small groups of 3 to 5 individuals to find a video and do a group-written reflection. This entire activity could be done online through a blogging website or a learning management system where participants are also asked to watch each other's videos and comment on each other's written reflections.

This activity may leave participants with more questions than answers, or even a sense of frustration, given the complexity of social issues and the processes needed to engage in societal-level change. Assure participants that these feelings are okay and worthy of exploring further on their own or with a trusted mentor. Often it is in this space of dissonance where participants will find the conviction to move forward with change-making efforts that they did not have the internal motivation to engage in previously. Another option is to have participants identify and investigate a change issue on campus and invite student leaders to the classroom for a follow-up discussion of the complexity of the change project.

An understanding of privilege and power is useful in processing this activity. Who is identifying the social issue? Does it include people within the community or outside of the community? Have the individuals within the community been involved in the change process? How do individual and group assumptions influence the perceptions related to social issues and proposed changes?

> Supplemental Readings

Fullan, M. (2001). *Leading in a culture of change.* San Francisco, CA: Jossey-Bass.

Fullan, M. (2011). *Change leader: Learning to do what matters most.* San Francisco, CA: Jossey-Bass.

Heifetz, R. A., & Linsky, M. (2002). *Leadership on the line: Staying alive through the dangers of leading*. Boston, MA: Harvard Business School Press.

Kegan, R., & Lahey, L. L. (2009). *Immunity to change: How to overcome it and unlock potential in yourself and your organization*. Boston, MA: Harvard Business Press.

Kotter, J. P. (1996). *Leading change*. Boston, MA: Harvard Business School Press.

Kouzes J. M., & Posner, B.Z. (2009). To lead, create a shared vision. *Harvard Business Review, 87*, 20–21. Available online at https://hbr.org/2009/01/to-lead-create-a-shared-vision

Shankman, M. L., Allen, S. J., & Haber-Curran, P. (2015). *Emotionally intelligent leadership: A guide for students* (2nd ed.). San Francisco, CA: Jossey-Bass.

Wallace, D. F. (2009). *This is water: Some thoughts, delivered on a significant occasion, about living a compassionate life*. New York, NY: Little, Brown and Company.

Wallace, D. F. (2013). This is water. *Kenyon College Alumni Bulletin, 35*(2). Available online at http://bulletin-archive.kenyon.edu/x4276.html

❯ Media

Derek Sivers (2009 November). TED Talk: Weird, or just different. Retrieved from: www.ted.com/talks/derek_sivers_weird_or_just_different

Alice Goffman (2015 March). TED Talk: How we're priming some kids for college - and others for prison. Retrieved from: www.ted.com/talks/alice_goffman_college_or_prison_two_destinies_one_blatant_injustice

Ken Robinson (2006 February). TED Talk: Do schools kill creativity? Retrieved from: www.ted.com/talks/ken_robinson_says_schools_kill_creativity

Leymah Gbowee (2012 March). TED Talk: Unlock the intelligence, passion, greatness of girls. Retrieved from: www.ted.com/talks/leymah_gbowee_unlock_the_intelligence_passion_greatness_of_girls

Jessica Jackley (2010 July). TED Talk: Poverty, money – and love. Retrieved from: www.ted.com/talks/jessica_jackley_poverty_money_and_love

Al Gore (2008 March). TED Talk: New thinking on the climate crisis. Retrieved from: www.ted.com/talks/al_gore_s_new_thinking_on_the_climate_crisis

LeaderShape, Inc.: www.leadershape.org

Change.org: www.change.org

❯ Suggested Questions for Discussions or Assignments

- What is a change you would like to promote in an organization or community of which you are a part? Do others in your organization or community see this change as a priority?
- What is something you could change about yourself that would make you more effective at leadership in groups?
- What organic change metaphors do you find yourself drawn to? Can you think of an example from your experience working in groups that was like that metaphor?
- What role has resistance played in the advancement or stagnation of a change effort in an organization with which you are involved?
- Consider a personal change goal that you have tried to make but did not maintain. What mental models might be at work that you should address?
- Consider a change goal you would like to make at the group or community level. Depict the systemic influences on that issue through a drawing like a mind-map.

❯ References

Allen, K. E., & Cherrey, C. (2000). *Systemic leadership: Enriching the meaning of our work.* Lanham, MD: University Press of America.

Bridges, W. (2003). *Managing transitions: Making the most of change* (2nd ed.). Cambridge, MA: Perseus.

Boyce, M. (2003). Organizational learning is essential to achieving and sustaining change in higher education. *Innovative Higher Education, 28*, 119–136. doi: 10.1023/B:IHIE.0000006287.69207.00

Dweck, C. S. (2006). *Mindset: The new psychology of success.* New York, NY: Random House.

Eckel, P., Hill, B., & Green, M. (1998). *On change: En route to transformation.* Washington, DC: American Council on Education.

Heifetz, R. A., Grashow, A., &; Linsky, M. (2009). *The practice of adaptive leadership: Tools and tactics for changing your organization and the world.* Boston, MA: Harvard Business Press.

Heifetz, R. A., &; Laurie, D. L. (1997). The work of leadership. *Harvard Business Review, 75*, 124–134. Retrieved from: https://hbr.org/2001/12/the-work-of-leadership

Heifetz, R. A., &; Linsky, M. (2002). *Leadership on the line: Staying alive through the dangers of leading.* Boston, MA: Harvard Business School Press.

Hultman, K. (1998). *Making change irresistible: Overcoming resistance to change in your organization*. Palo Alto, CA: Davies-Black.

Kegan, R., & Lahey, L. L. (2009). *Immunity to change: How to overcome it and unlock potential in yourself and your organization*. Boston, MA: Harvard Business Press.

Senge, P. M. (2006). *The fifth discipline: The art and practice of the learning organization*. New York, NY: Doubleday/Currency.

Senge, P. M. (2014). *The dance of change: The challenges to sustaining momentum in a learning organization*. New York, NY: Crown Publishing Group.

Wagner, W. (2017). Change. In Komives, S. R., Wagner, W., & Associates, *Leadership for a better world* (2nd Ed.; pp. 201–232). San Francisco, CA: Jossey-Bass.

Wallace, D. F. (2009). *This Is Water: Some thoughts, delivered on a significant occasion, about living a compassionate life*. New York, NY: Little, Brown and Company.

Melissa L. Rocco is an instructor, curriculum developer, and advisor in the Leadership Studies Program at the University of Maryland, College Park. Melissa is a contributing author to the Jossey-Bass *New Directions for Student Leadership* series and *Leadership Theory: A Facilitator's Guide for Cultivating Critical Perspectives*. She is also a doctoral candidate in the Student Affairs Concentration in the Counseling, Higher Education, and Special Education program at the University of Maryland, College Park and she earned her master's degree in higher education and student affairs at The Ohio State University.

Chapter 13

Social Change

Danielle S. Kleist & Jordyn C. Wright

> ## Summary of Key Concepts

The concept of *Social Change* as the focus of the Social Change Model (SCM) of Leadership Development can be discussed as the reasoning for individuals and groups who are making a greater impact for the betterment of society. Change can happen on many levels in various ways. An individual can make the biggest change when assessing the impact on the greater good and working in collaboration with others. For example, in *Leadership for a Better World* (2nd edition), social change is described as viewing a problem by researching the root cause and not just looking at the surface level (Wagner, 2017). In addition to a focus on root cause problem solving, social change is community-oriented and occurs via collaborative relationships among stakeholders.

For Social Change to occur, it needs to be a positive change that benefits a larger whole. Social change focuses on the positive impact that transforms society through change agents. During social change, the root cause needs to be addressed. *Root cause* is defined as the underlying source that defines a situation and normally surfaces after reflection. Wagner (2017) describes this via a metaphor of saving babies drowning in a river. Individuals rescue the babies and provide resources to save them, but in order to accomplish social change, they need to look upstream to identify why the babies are even in the river in the first place. By solving the issue of why the babies are in the river, this will make an impact on a larger problem and prevent future occurrences of drowning.

An inherent challenge in advocating for positive change is defining what is considered "positive." Within a group, individuals will have distinct ideas of what outcomes are preferred and what processes will best lead to that outcome. Groups, teams, and organizations often have very different aims (that they consider positive), which may be in conflict with one another. "Positive" should be viewed with an awareness of both outcome and process, as well as competing demands and goals. Furthermore, there is privilege and power associated with who gets to define what is "positive." Considering dimensions of privilege and power when working toward social change is important in making sure the change is valuable and desired by most individuals and groups within a given community.

As individuals, groups, and communities work toward social change and enact socially responsible leadership, it is also important to consider possible pitfalls of engaging in this important work. These pitfalls include *assimilation*, in which "helpers" try to make others more like them; *paternalism*, in which "helpers" assume they know what is best and do not include community members in the decision-making process; ignoring the historical and political context; using a *deficit-based approach* that focuses on perceived problems rather than community assets; ignoring cultural differences; and confusing social change with public relations (Wagner, 2017). When engaging in social change and socially responsible leadership, it is possible to avoid these pitfalls and still make mistakes. Good intentions do not always lead to the desired impact and a perfect solution will not always be achieved, but these fears should not keep us from working to better the world. By working together, implementing a growth mind-set (Dweck, 2006), and employing the C values of the Social Change Model, it is possible to create change and lead in a socially responsible manner.

> Activities Overview

The five activities provided in this chapter will help demonstrate social change at the individual, group, and societal level. The first activity, *Actions on the Line*, will help an individual assess their personal values, and how those personal values connect to personal action. Participants will create values-based action statements and recognize how their approach compares to others. They will understand the importance of self-awareness by seeing the variety of approaches to change that exist.

In Activity Two, *Social Change Groups*, participants will learn about group social change. Participants will work in small groups to learn how others developed their values and identify how groups and the people one associates with have influenced a person's perspective. In the third activity, *Start with the Basics*, participants will reflect on specific problems and assets within their organizations and communities to better understand deficit and asset-based approaches to community development. Activity Four, *Root Causes: From a Tree to a Forest*, focuses on identifying root causes and the connected nature of each social issue. The last activity, *Paradigms of Service*, brings these concepts together and asks participants to reflect on past service or volunteer experiences.

Estimated Time
Activity One: *Actions on the Line*, 30 minutes
Activity Two: *Social Change Groups*, 60 minutes
Activity Three: *Start with the Basics*, 60 minutes
Activity Four: *Root Causes: From a Tree to a Forest*, 30 to 60 minutes
Activity Five: *Paradigms of Service*, 20 minutes

⟩ Learning Activities

Activity One: Actions on the Line

Time: 30 minutes

Learning Outcomes   Participants will

- Be able to express their personal values-based actions to the group.
- Learn others' personal qualities through discussion.
- Understand the importance of self-awareness.

Materials
- Small sticky notes (same size and color for each participant) or slips of paper
- Writing utensils
- Small container to hold values-based action statements

Detailed Instructions   Prior to the activity, prepare 2 to 3 values-based action statements that will be intermixed with the participants' individual values-based action statements. For example, "I choose to spend time with friends over family," "I would intervene during a physical conflict between two strangers in public," or "I avoid using disposable paper products in my home to reduce my carbon footprint."

Inform participants that they will be discussing values-based action statements and emphasize that no statement is wrong or better than another. If at any time a participant does not feel comfortable, let the participant know they may step out of the activity and/or room.

- Have each participant write down one values-based action statement. Provide examples if necessary.
- Collect the statements in a container to easily mix the statements.
- Have all the participants stand in the middle of the room.
- Designate the room into two sections (left side and right side).

Inform participants that the values-based action statements will be read; Participants who agree with the statement should go to the left side of the room, and participants who disagree or think the opposite should go to the right side. One side must be chosen, and participants are not allowed to stand in the middle between sides. Allow for silence while the statements are read, and when participants are selecting sides. Disclose to participants that additional values-based action statements have been intermixed with their own statements.

- Read each values-based action statement as follows: "Move to the left side if (insert values-based action statement) and move to the right side if (state opposite of values-based action statement)."
- After all of the participants have selected a side, instruct the group to look around and observe the 2 sides, in silence. Remind participants to not make comments or discuss what they observe.
- After going through all of the values-based action statements, have participants return to their original spots and start group discussion.

Here are some processing questions for leading the large group discussion:

- What did you observe during this activity?
- Was it difficult to select a side?
- Did anything surprise you?
- If provided with these statements again, would you change your side?
- How would you apply this to (insert theme/reasoning for having activity)?
- What do you do when your values come into conflict? What do you do when your actions conflict with your espoused values?

These questions are provided to start the conversation. However, observe the group dynamics as well as the responses to the beginning questions. This will allow the debriefing to be fluid and participant responses to carry the conversation.

Facilitator Notes   This activity can be facilitated in large or small groups. However, it is most effective in groups larger than 15 participants. It is important to use the same color, size, and kind of paper for each participant. This is to reassure participants that their values-based action statements are added into the large group anonymously. By doing this, the participants will feel more secure in selecting a side of the room during a potentially vulnerable activity.

Activity Two: Social Change Groups

Time: 60 minutes

Learning Outcomes   Participants will

- Identify how perspective and background play a part in the decision-making process.
- Learn to consider others' perspectives and backgrounds and how they can affect social change.
- Increase personal understanding of their world and community.
- Recognize how social change affects their lives.

Detailed Instructions   Conduct a quick activity to split participants into multiple groups for small group discussion. Here are some examples of ways to split participants into small groups:

- Only child, small family, large family
- Political parties
- Currently living in hometown, born somewhere else and grew up in current location, recently moved to area
- Family from current location, family grew up somewhere else
- Age of participants
- Cultural background/demographics
- Grew up well off, middle class, lower-income
- Part of a fraternity or sorority, lived in the residence halls

Allow participants 5 to 10 minutes to discuss issues that could influence a person's perspective based on their group identification. Have each group identify a note-taker to record comments for large group discussion. In the small groups, the groups will discuss social change.

Recommended discussion questions include:
- What were the social issues in your community?
- What affected your views on society?
- How has your view of the world changed from when you were a child to the present?
- What current events do you remember as a child and how did they affect you and your family?
- How have your family dynamics changed over time?
- Who was your childhood hero? Who is your hero now? Are they the same? Why or why not?
- Did you grow up watching or reading the news? How did your experience watching or reading the news (or not) affect your experiences growing up?

After 5 to 10 minutes (time may vary based on participants), split participants into different small groups, using new identifiers this time. Have each group identify a note-taker to record comments for large group discussion. After the second breakout, and once the small groups have discussed for 5 to 10 minutes, bring participants together as into the large group. Begin a debriefing with the large group based on the small group discussions.

Recommended large group discussion questions:
- How did your views compare to others in the group?
- What was surprising to you about other groups? Did you have assumptions about what a group might or might not care about?
- Was there a topic that proved to resonate more than another?
- What did you notice about yourself?
- Based on all of the areas, what area do you feel has most affected your sense of social change agency?
- How would you collaborate now with people with different views?
- Did any of your backgrounds have a common purpose? How has your common purpose changed as you have grown?

If time permits, break the large group into smaller groups 2 more times, and engage in large discussion again to help participants reflect on various dialogues.

By the end of the activity, participants should be able to see how different backgrounds provide unique perspectives. However, people with different backgrounds do not necessarily mean their views will automatically be different. Interactions between different groups can affect individual ideologies around social change.

Facilitator Notes   This activity can be done with large or small groups. However, this activity is most successful with at least 10 participants. Make sure that small group configurations do not repeat during different breakout sessions (if this happens, the facilitator may need to move participants around). The facilitator should keep in mind already-identified demographics of the group, and consider splitting the participants that way. The more diverse the groups, the more unique perspectives the participants will have on social change. This is an opportunity to discuss the intersection of privilege and power in communities as well as varying perspectives on "positive" change.

Activity Three: Start with the Basics

Time: 60 minutes

Learning Outcomes   Participants will

- Be able to work collaboratively as a group to discuss internal problems and identify assets.
- Learn ways to identify root cause(s) for a specific situation.
- Develop skills to be able to identify the basic issues of a situation.
- Consider the differences between deficit approaches and asset-based approaches to community development.

Materials
- Sticky notes
- Writing utensils
- 2 containers to collect sticky notes

Detailed Instructions Participants will each write a problem on a small sticky note that they would like to examine within their organization or community. Have each participant fold the sticky note and place it into a communal container. Once every participant has added a problem into the container, select someone to blindly select a sticky note for the group to discuss as a whole.

Instruct the group(s) to review the problem and determine how the problem originated. How does this affect the organization, and what can the group do to resolve the problem? If there is time, the group could select a second problem to discuss. (*15 to 20 minutes*)

After the participants have determined they are finished, the facilitator should hold a discussion with the entire group.

Initial processing questions for group discussion:
- Did everyone agree this was a problem within the organization or community?
- How did you begin discussing the problem?
- How did you determine what the root cause of the problem was?
- What was the impact on the organization or community?
- Did the group discover a solution to the problem?

Next, have participants consider an asset in their organization or community. They should then write that asset on a sticky note, and place the note in a separate container. Once every participant has added an asset into the container, select an individual to blindly select a sticky note for the group to discuss as a whole. Instruct the group(s) to review the asset and determine how the asset originated. How does this affect the organization, and what can the group do to leverage this asset? If there is time, the group could select a second asset. (*15 to 20 minutes*)

After the participants have determined they are finished, the facilitator should hold a discussion with the entire group.

Further processing session questions for group discussion:
- Did everyone agree this was an asset within the organization or community?

- How did you begin discussing the asset?
- How did you determine what the benefit of the asset was?
- What was the impact on the organization or community?
- Did the group discover how this asset might be part of a community solution?

Once participants have discussed problems and assets within the organizations or communities, engage in a discussion conversation related to the different approaches to social change. A *deficit-based approach* begins with a problem, whereas an *asset-based approach* begins with the assumption that local assets are the key to sustainable social change. Here are some discussion questions to begin the conversation.

Discussion Questions   The following discussion questions can be used to guide a debrief of the activity:

- What differences emerged when considering problems and assets? Were some problems also assets, and were some assets also problems? Why or why not?
- How can you distinguish between a deficit-based approach to community development and identifying a root cause? How might a root cause be considered an asset?
- What are the systemic challenges to achieving desired social change that are influenced by both problems and assets within an organization or community?
- What are examples within historical social movements that use a deficit-based approach? An asset-based approach?

Facilitator Notes   To help participants visualize the problems, you may have participants create an idea web for the problem on a whiteboard, sheet of paper, or butcher paper. Have participants write the problem in the middle and circle the issue. Darting out from the middle problem, participants will write what the group discusses as causes to the problem. Participants may continue this pattern to help them determine what initially caused the problem. Participants may also find it helpful to break down the problem by listing the people associated with the problem, and/or concepts to help them find where the problem originated. The same can be done for the assets.

Participants may notice that there are problems to the problems (or problems to the assets, or assets to the assets, or even assets to the problem!). As a facilitator, do not share with participants that this "secondary problem finding" (or asset finding) is part of the process to discovering the root cause. It would be beneficial for the facilitator to take notes on the group's dynamics, and share any observations of the group process during the processing discussion.

Facilitators can also process this activity using the Five Whys developed by Rick Ross (1994). Komives, Lucas, and McMahon (2013) describe this approach as:

> Ask yourself the most simple of questions, such as, 'Why does your organization (or group or community) exist?' This question is relevant whether it is asked about student government, a service organization, the chess club, a residence hall floor or house government, a fraternity or sorority, or a club related to your major. Probe deeply. Now take the reason you have given and ask why that answer is important. Take the answer to that second Why? and ask Why? again. Do this until you have asked Why? a total of five times. Doing this helps you get closer to the essence of why the group exists. (p. 392)

The Five Whys approach works to help identify root causes as well as assets within an organization or community.

Activity Four: Root Causes: From a Tree to a Forest[1]

Time: 30 to 60 minutes

Learning Outcomes   Participants will

- Identify the root causes of social issues and distinguish those from the surface-level issues.

---

[1] Adapted from Doerr, E. (2010). What is social change? In W. Wagner, D. T. Ostick, S. R. Komives, & Associates (Eds.). *Leadership for a better world: Instructor manual* (p. 10–31). A publication of the National Clearinghouse for Leadership Programs. San Francisco: CA: Jossey-Bass.

- Focus on how they can be involved in specific change for that issue.
- Identify the interconnectedness of issues by demonstrating the shared root causes of various issues.

Materials
- Markers
- Large paper (1 paper per group), or a prepared worksheet that includes an image of a tree with leaves, a trunk, and roots
- 1 extra-large piece of paper prepared with a large tree that includes leaves, a trunk, and roots

Detailed Instructions   Part 1 – Root Causes Tree

Convene participants in a circle (for a small group), or divide participants into small groups of 3 to 5 members (for a large group). Pass out markers and paper. Ask participants to draw leaves, a trunk, and the roots of a tree on their paper. (Alternatively, distribute a worksheet that has a pre-drawn tree.)

Have participants discuss amongst themselves some of the social issues that they see in their community or around the world. Ask them to identify one issue that is important to all of the people in the group and ask them to write that issue on the trunk of the tree.

Ask the participants to think about some of the root causes to that problem. For example, for homelessness, root causes might include living wage, resources, healthcare, social inequality, or natural disasters. Have them write these root causes on the roots of the tree.

Ask the participants to think of possible solutions to the problems written on the roots, and ask them to write these solutions on the leaves of the tree.

Ask the participants to think of ways they can possibly be a part of meeting the needs related to the root causes. Have them write that on the side of the paper next to the trunk. Emphasize that these are ways to meet the needs of the root causes, and not anything else.

Ask each group to present their issue and root causes. Have the group convene in a circle so everyone can see each other and begin discussing the questions listed below as a group. The facilitator should write the themes and discussion issues that come up on a flip chart or whiteboard and could use the extra-large tree as an example for the large group.

Part One Discussion Questions

- Were there any themes that emerged amongst the root causes? What were they, and why do you think they came up?
- In looking at the root causes, what do you think the "surface-level" issues might be?
- How is that different from a root cause?
- Do you think it is better to only work on the root causes and not just at the surface? Do you think you can do them together? If so, how?
- Do these root causes seem easy to combat?
- Do the ideas that you brainstormed for meeting the needs of the root causes seem feasible or easy to do?
- How can you get started to combat the root causes of the problem?
- How is this activity relevant when discussing social change?

Part 2 – Root Causes Forest

If the large group creates one tree, begin discussion about what other issues might share the same root causes. It may be useful to do two root cause trees and demonstrate the interconnectedness between them.

Have participants post their root cause trees around the room, and then move around the room taking note of the root causes of the other trees. After a few minutes, begin a discussion about the interconnectedness of root causes, using the questions listed below.

Part Two Discussion Questions

- Did any of you see trees/issues that had the same root cause as your issue?
- Do you see how those issues might be connected?
- What does this mean in terms of social change?
- What happens if we only looked at the one tree? Do we see the forest if we concentrate on that?
- How does the forest look?

Facilitator Notes   This activity works best in a large room so that people can move around. When working in large groups, the facilitator should have enough space so that participants can work in smaller groups without distracting the other groups.

If a group has come together to decide on how to work on a specific problem, the activity can be followed up with an action plan of sorts in order to begin addressing the problem. Understanding the root cause is the first step to achieving change.

The issues that are brainstormed can be adapted to the learning context. Homelessness is a good example for participants in a social justice education context. However, there might be more relevant community issues for participants in a student government association. The issue can be something that participants have already decided to work on together in that case.

Activity Five: Paradigms of Service[2]

Time: 20 minutes

Learning Outcomes   Participants will

- Reflect on past service experiences to explore social change elements and possible pitfalls.

Materials
- Worksheet with activity questions

Detailed Instructions   Ask each participant to think of a past experience engaging as a volunteer for a social cause or community organization. These can be any type of engagement, from one-time activities to prolonged engagements. Explain Keith Morton's (1995) classic work, *The Irony of Service*, to describe three forms of service: *Charity* (work that addresses immediate needs); *Projects* (work that builds the capacity or efficiency of groups who attend to immediate needs); and *Social Change* (work aimed at

---

[2] Developed by Daniel T. Ostick

changing the systems that cause the needs). Remind participants that one category is not better or worse than another, and that what distinguishes the experience, according to Morton (1995), is the level of "thickness," or understanding of root causes and relationships within the community. Ask each participant to identify in which category their experience belongs, and their level of thickness for that experience.

Hand out a worksheet to each participant with the following questions and give participants 10 to 15 minutes to complete it. Explain that these may be difficult or impossible questions for them to answer:

Creating Change

- What was the long-term impact of your activity?
- What unintended consequences might have resulted?
- Was your presence actually maintaining the structures of inequity by mitigating the impact of the issue? Why or why not?

Root Causes of Social Issues

- How did the situation come to be this way?
- How do economic, political, and social systems and cultural values allow the issue to continue?
- What local, state, national, or international policies contribute to the issue?
- Why does the general public accept the ongoing existence of this issue?

Collaboration and Relationships

- Who else is affected by this issue? Who else has a stake in the outcome?
- Who has access to the resources needed to address the issue?
- Who has influence on the rules (e.g. policies, legal requirements, and enforcement of existing law)?

After participants have completed their worksheets, facilitate a large group discussion, using the following questions.

Discussion Questions   The following discussion questions can be used to guide a debrief of the activity:

- Was the worksheet hard to complete? Why?

- Was the worksheet easier or harder to complete depending on whether your experience was Charity, Project, or Change work? Was your experience thick or thin? Why would that matter?
- If your project experience was thin, how could it have become thicker?

Facilitator Notes   An understanding of Morton's (1995) research is useful in facilitating this activity. He presents an initial approach to charity, project, and change as a continuum, but then refines his approach to be paradigms of service that vary by level of thickness. Under the paradigm approach, Charity, Project, and Change can all be effective approaches to service if they approach the work with sustained relationships and a root cause orientation.

If this activity is for a class, or if time permits, it can be adapted to encourage participants to create and engage in a social change project together. The project can be designed using these same guiding questions and then, during and after the engagement, can be used to help participants reflect on their experiences. If time does not permit, participants can also use the questions to design an imagined experience that reflects the values of social change.

❯ Supplemental Readings

Dugan, J. P. (2017). *Leadership theory: Cultivating critical perspectives*. San Francisco, CA: Jossey-Bass.

Evans, M., & Knight Abowitz, K. (Eds.). (2015). *New Directions for Student Leadership: No. 148. Engaging youth in leadership for social and political change*. San Francisco, CA: Jossey-Bass.

Fullan, M. (2001). *Leading in a culture of change*. San Francisco, CA: Jossey-Bass.

Goodwin, J., & Jasper, J. (2015). *The social movements reader: Cases and concepts*. Malden, MA: Wiley/Blackwell.

Jones, E., Haenfler, R., & Johnson, B. (2007). *The better world handbook*. Gabriola Island, British Columbia: New Society Publishers.

Kotter, J. P. (2002). *The heart of change: Real-life stories of how people change their organizations*. Boston, MA: Harvard Business School Press.

Loeb, P. R. (Ed.). (2004). *The impossible will take a little while: A citizen's guide to hope in a time of fear*. New York, NY: Basic Books.

Morton, K. (1995). The irony of service: Charity, project and social change in service-learning. *Michigan Journal of Community Service Learning, 2*(1), 19–32. Available online at: http://hdl.handle.net/2027/spo.3239521.0002.102

❯ Media

Parag Khanna (2016 February). TED Talk: How megacities are changing the map of the world. Retrieved from: www.ted.com/talks/parag_khanna_how_megacities_are_changing_the_map_of_the_world#t-362279

Derek Sivers (2010 February). TED Talk: How to Start a Movement. Retrieved from: www.ted.com/talks/derek_sivers_how_to_start_a_movement#t-141255

Drew Dudley (2010 September). TEDx Talk: Everyday leadership. Retrieved from: www.ted.com/talks/drew_dudley_everyday_leadership

More TED Talk topics on Social Change: www.ted.com/topics/social+change

Change.org: www.change.org

Taking It Global: www.tigweb.org

Volunteer Match: www.volunteermatch.org

Do Something: www.dosomething.org

Barefoot Collective: www.barefootguide.org

❯ Suggested Questions for Discussions or Assignments

- In what ways have you been involved in social change efforts? What social issues or what communities are you drawn to?
- Can you think of an example of an organization that you have been involved with or not, that did a particularly good job of collaborating with others and addressing the root causes of issues?
- What is your motivation of being involved in social change efforts? What holds you back?
- Describe someone you would consider a hero in terms of their commitment to making a positive difference for others. In what ways can you see yourself being like them? In

what ways does their achievement intimidate you? Who are the individuals who help your hero accomplish their goals?

- Think of a group you belong to that is not defined by its goal to do social change, such as a residence hall community, sports team, or academic club. How does that organization affect its members? How does it affect others in its community? How could that organization practice socially responsible leadership?
- Do you think leaders create social movements or do social movements create leaders? How have your experiences with leadership shaped your motivation to work for the common good? How have your experiences trying to make a difference for the common good affected how you approach leadership?
- With what groups or individuals do you have influence? In what arenas do you have the power to have a positive influence? How could you utilize your current influence to create change on an issue that matters to you?
- How do the intersections of privilege, power, and oppression influence movements for social change?

> ## References

Doerr, E. (2010). What is social change? In W. Wagner, D. T. Ostick, S. R. Komives, & Associates (Eds.), *Leadership for a better world: Instructor manual* (pp. 10–31). A publication of the National Clearinghouse for Leadership Programs. San Francisco, CA: Jossey-Bass.

Dweck, C. S. (2006). *Mindset: The new psychology of success.* New York, NY: Random House.

Higher Education Research Institute [HERI] (1996). *A social change model of leadership development (Version III).* Los Angeles, CA: University of California Los Angeles, Higher Education Research Institute.

Komives, S. R., Lucas, N., & McMahon, T. R. (2013). *Exploring leadership: For college students who want to make a difference* (3rd ed.). San Francisco, CA: Jossey-Bass.

Morton, K. (1995). The irony of service: Charity, project and social change in service-learning. *Michigan Journal of Community Service Learning, 2*(1), 19–32. Retrieved from: http://hdl.handle.net/2027/spo.3239521.0002.102

Ross, R. (1994). The Five Whys. In P. Senge, *The fifth discipline fieldbook* (pp. 108–112). New York, NY: Doubleday.

Wagner, W. (2017). Examining social change. In S. R. Komives, W. Wagner, & Associates, *Leadership for a better world: Understanding the social change model of leadership development* (2nd Ed.; pp. 233–260). San Francisco, CA: Jossey-Bass.

Danielle S. Kleist is the Director of Student Life at Washington State University Tri-Cities and a consultant for Proof Leadership Group. Prior to her current role, Danielle was the Director of Orientation and Commuter Student Involvement at the University of Miami and the Assistant Director of Educational Programs and the NASPA Foundation at NASPA – Student Affairs Administrators in Higher Education. Her career has been focused on developing leaders at multiple levels and evaluating the success of programs and organizations. Danielle received her Bachelor of Science from Central Washington University and Master of Education from the University of Nevada, Las Vegas.

Jordyn C. Wright is the Student Financial and Support Services Manager at Washington State University Tri-Cities. Jordyn has worked to develop an on-campus food bank, tax services, and free legal advice for students. She previously worked as the Assistant Greek Advisor at the University of Idaho. Jordyn received her Master of Education in Counseling and Human Services and her Bachelor of Science in Political Science from the University of Idaho.

Chapter 14

Applying the Model

Daniel T. Ostick & Kristan Cilente Skendall

Summary of the Key Concepts

The Social Change Model (SCM) of Leadership Development provides an evidence-based approach designed for use by a variety of leaders and groups. Any application of the model should identify the problem or social issue, help members to clarify values, research important knowledge and knowledge gaps, and enact accountability.

In identifying the problem or justice issue, leaders may find it helpful to define what their initiative will and will not entail. Socially responsible leadership applications may entail some or all of the following elements: societal principles of fairness; fair decision-making processes and policies; and social inclusion or ways that societal members treat each other (Jost & Kay, 2010). By carefully identifying the desired justice outcome, leaders can better chart plans that support change.

It is also important to clarify values of group members and identify unique talents that contribute to the identified change. Tying specific values to particular contributions will allow team members to thrive and contribute.

No one person knows everything, so clarifying knowledge and knowledge gaps will help the group ensure that their plans are relevant. A group should gather as much information as possible to understand the issue from personal, community, national, and global perspectives. This knowledge will help clarify group purpose and assist in creating real and useful change.

Assessment and accountability considerations are critical to avoid the trap of changing for the sake of change without having systemic impact. Leaders should begin a change process by asking and answering the question, "How will we know if we have been successful?" Clarifying purpose upfront should be paired with the identification of evidence and critical conversations about authentic success.

> Activities Overview

The activities in this chapter, if completed in order, will walk participants through the process of social change, from identifying purpose, clarifying talents and unique contributions, developing networks, identifying knowledge gaps, and crafting assessment plans.

Activity One, *Begin with the End in Mind*, asks participants to develop metrics of success related to specific goals. The second activity, *Talent Blueprint*, leads participants through the process of identifying the skills and talents they possess, and how to tie those skills into helping their cause. Activity Three, *My Networks*, helps participants identify the individuals and groups that have a stake in their groups or mission and may be supportive of their endeavors. Activity Four, *You Don't Know What You Don't Know*, asks participants to think about the important information critical to working on their issue, and to identify where gaps may lie in their knowledge. The final activity, *Knowledge Hunt*, encourages participants to quickly gather information, offering an easy way to build their knowledge base.

Estimated Time
Activity One: *Begin with the End in Mind*, 30 minutes
Activity Two: *Talent Blueprint*, 20 minutes

Activity Three: *My Networks*, 30 minutes
Activity Four: *You Don't Know What You Don't Know*, 30 minutes
Activity Five: *Knowledge Hunt*, 20 minutes

› Learning Activities

Activity One: Begin with the End in Mind

Time: 30 minutes

Learning Outcomes   Participants will

- Clarify the purpose of their social change.
- Identify measures of success.

Materials
- Paper
- Writing utensils

Detailed Instructions   Instruct each participant to write the following on a sheet of paper:

- TOPIC (at the top)
- PURPOSE STATEMENT DRAFT (in the middle)
- METRICS (at the bottom)

    Define each of these terms for the group as follows:

- *Topic*—This is the general issue. For instance, shoreline restoration or childhood literacy.
- *Purpose Statement Draft*—This is the individual's specific goal or vision. For instance, increasing childhood literacy or support efforts for shoreline restoration. (*Note*: these purpose statements are vague on purpose.)

- *Metrics*—These are very specific measures or numbers that answer the question, "How will we know if we succeeded?" While the Social Change Model describes the process toward social change, it is important for participants to be clear on how they can really know if they are creating real change.

Note: Participants should work on this task individually for 10 to 15 minutes, with the facilitator walking around to answer questions and help participants who are struggling.

Next, ask participants to turn their paper over and write "PURPOSE STATEMENT DRAFT 2" at the top. Ask them to rewrite their purpose statement draft into a more concrete purpose statement by using the measures of success.

Next, ask them to evaluate their purpose statement using S.M.A.R.T. goals, as follows:

- SPECIFIC—The who, what, when, where, why, and which. Is the goal clear and unambiguous?
- MEASURABLE—Can the goal be tracked for progress?
- ATTAINABLE—Can the goal be accomplished? Is it out of reach (more like a vision), or too simple (more like a step toward a strong goal)?
- RELEVANT—If the goal is accomplished, will it meet the needs identified? Is this the desired goal?
- TIMELY—When will the goal be accomplished? Does it give a sense of urgency?

Next, ask participants to write on a new piece of paper "FINAL PURPOSE STATEMENT." Ask them to rewrite their purpose statement again, using the feedback gathered from the S.M.A.R.T. goals information.

Ask for a volunteer who would like to share their process and purpose statement with the group, as an example of the small group work still to come. As the volunteer shares their process and purpose statement, the facilitator and group should ask clarifying questions that illuminate information about the purpose statement and its relationship to goals and assessment.

At this point, place participants into small groups in order to share and critique each other's purpose statements, and to provide any additional clarification (similar to the large group process, but in smaller groups this time).

Facilitator Notes   It will be important for the facilitator to stress the importance of these steps in the social change process. Failure to spend time defining a strong purpose statement or vision can result in less change, claiming success when unwarranted, or accomplishing unintended changes. While the model speaks to the process of change, that process is toward a particular end, so that particular end needs to be clearly understood and articulated.

Activity Two: Talent Blueprint

Time: 20 minutes

Learning Outcomes   Participants will

- Be able to connect their unique talents to causes of interest.

Materials
- Paper
- Writing utensils

Detailed Instructions   Prepare a list of issues or causes ahead of time, or brainstorm a list of issues of interest with participants. Examples might include homelessness, food insecurity, recycling, child abuse or neglect, racism, illiteracy, and so on.

Ask each participant to identify one skill or talent they possess (possibly identified through a Consciousness of Self activity from Chapter 5, such as *Activity Two: Bag It*). If participants are struggling to identify talents, help them brainstorm. Talents may include public speaking, organizational skills, finance, facilitation, writing, or graphic design, to name just a few.

Assign or ask participants to select an issue in which they are interested. Then, ask each person to connect their talent to that issue in five unique and creative ways. Asking them to come up with five ways will force participants to think beyond the obvious.

If this seems too challenging for the group, provide a personal example to illustrate, or work through an example as a group. For instance, to connect the issue of LGBT rights to the talent of creative writing, you could:

- Design and edit an LGBT creative writing journal for your campus
- Submit poetry about the LGBT experience to campus publications or local blogs
- Write an editorial about LGBT experiences or rights for the campus newspaper
- Edit the monthly newsletter from the campus LGBT student organization
- Lead or speak at a rally, using your unique voice or submitted article

If time permits, have each participant share some or all of their examples. If time does not permit, have participants share in small groups of 3 to 5 participants.

Facilitator Notes   Facilitators can make this activity abstract or more relevant to the needs of the group, as appropriate. If leading a diverse group at a retreat with a wide variety of interests, it may be better to use a range of examples. If working with an intact group with a shared vision, the examples can be more directly relevant to their efforts.

This activity can also be done as a worksheet, with columns headings titled "Issue," "Talent," and "Unique Contribution," allowing participants to tie a variety of issues to a variety of talents.

Activity Three: My Networks

Time: 30 minutes

Learning Outcomes   Participants will

- Identify important contributors to their issue.
- Develop a map of personal networks.

Materials

- Paper
- Writing utensils

Detailed Instructions   In this activity, students will develop a map of their personal networks, particularly in relation to a topic of interest.

Ask participants to write their name in the center of a sheet of paper. From their name, they should draw five spokes leading outwards. These spokes should be labeled "OTHER GROUPS," "CRITICAL CHAMPIONS," "EXPERTS," "CHEERSQUAD," and "STAKEHOLDERS." Define these terms for the group as follows:

- *Other Groups*—This would include any local, state, national, or international groups that either work on this issue, work on a related issue, or care about this issue.
- *Critical Champions*—This would include individuals who are critical to success. Their involvement would make an enormous difference to your success.
- *Experts*—This would include people you know who know the most about your issue. This might include professors, other students, or even heads of nonprofits or community organizations in your area.
- *Cheersquad*—This would include members of your support system; the individuals you look to for personal guidance, a listening ear, or just to de-stress.
- *Stakeholders*—This would include anyone who has a vested interest in your topic, both those who would be impacted, positively or negatively, and possibly those who would not wish you to succeed.

Participants should spend some time filling out their network maps, and encouraged to pair up and discuss their maps with others as they work to complete them. Once completed, lead the large group in a debriefing conversation, using the following general questions:

- Why would it be important to pay attention to these groups?
- Which spokes were easy to complete? Which were difficult? What might this tell you about the work, issue, or process moving forward?

Depending on the size of the group, some or all of the networks could be shared aloud. As facilitator, make connections between different maps if you can. (For example, there may be possible overlap in Other Groups, even though the issues are different; Cheersquads may include a lot of family member roles, indicating the importance of family support; or Expert lists might be short, indicating some work needing to be done to locate these.)

Facilitator Notes   Consider creating premade worksheets with the network maps already designed, and the definitions listed below them if that would save time. Facilitators may also want to add additional spokes relevant to their situation (for instance, breaking up Other Groups into subsections like Nonprofits or Community Organizations, Student Organizations, and Campus Departments).

Activity Four: You Don't Know What You Don't Know

Time: 30 minutes

Learning Outcomes   Participants will

- Identify important questions to consider in pursuing their cause.
- Identify personal knowledge gaps.

Materials
- Large poster paper (1 sheet per person)
- Markers (1 per person)
- (*Optional:* Sticky notes)
- Tape (if poster paper is not self-adhesive)

Detailed Instructions   On large poster sheets, ask each participant to write their cause or purpose at the top. These can be general ("recycling") or specific ("I want there to be compost stations in every dining facility on campus"). These large sheets should be posted around the room.

For 20 minutes, participants should walk around the room and write on each other's sheets. They should write questions that they think would be important for the individual to answer as they pursue their issue. For instance, using the compost example, participants might write, "what can be composted?" or "are stations better than separating later?" or "what do you do with the compost?" or "is there a cost involved?" Remind participants that there are no right or wrong questions. Consider using sticky notes for this portion.

Next, each participant should go back to their personal sheet and read over all the questions. Ask them to mark each question with a marker, as follows:

- ***Star (*)***—I know this already.
- ***Square (■)***—I don't know the answer to this, but know how to find out.
- ***Question Mark (?)***—I don't know the answer to this, and I don't know how to find out.
- ***X (x)***—I don't need to know this (or at least I think I don't need to know this).

Then, facilitate a large group discussion about the experience, using the following discussion questions.

Discussion Questions   The following discussion questions can be used to guide a debrief of the activity:

- What kinds of marks were most common?
- Were you surprised by how many question marks you had? How might you move those into square or star territory?
- What did you learn from this? (*Note:* Responses may include that more ideas and involvement can create greater knowledge; that we can't know everything; or that we always have more to learn.)

Facilitator Notes   Depending on the group, this activity could also be done in small teams, if individuals have similar areas of interest.

Activity Five: Knowledge Hunt

Time: 20 minutes

Learning Outcomes   Participants will

- Engage in the process of answering questions and gathering information about their topic.
- Recognize that critical information can be found quickly.

Materials
- Internet-accessible devices

Detailed Instructions   Assign or ask each student to choose a topic of interest. Tell them they have only *10 minutes* to find the following:

- An online video clip that would educate others about the topic
- Two national or international organizations that work on that issue
- A local (or campus) group that would be a stakeholder
- A website dedicated to the issue
- A virtual or online group focused on the topic
- The answer to one of the questions you didn't know the answer to from the previous activity (if applicable)

Ask students to share 1 or 2 of the best resources they found. Remind students that critical and helpful information can be found without hours of searching. They just need to take a little time to find individuals, groups, and sites that can support their efforts. Ask students how they knew the organization or information was reliable, in order to reinforce the concept of information literacy and make sure that participants chose legitimate sources.

Facilitator Notes   This activity builds well from the previous activity, *You Don't Know What You Don't Know*, but can be used on its own. This activity can be assigned for participants to complete before the in-person group meeting, or as homework, but conducting it on-site reinforces that resources can be found quickly and easily. Remind participants that while information can be found quickly, it is important to vet resources, ensure information comes from a reliable source, and continue to update information over time.

› Supplemental Readings

Aaker, J. (2010). *The dragonfly effect: Quick, effective, and powerful ways to use social media to drive social change*. San Francisco, CA: Jossey-Bass.

Buschlen, E., & Dvorak, R. (2011). The social change model as pedagogy: Examining undergraduate leadership growth. *Journal of Leadership Development, 10*(2), 38–56. doi: 10.12806/v10/i2/rf2

Dugan, J. P. (2006). Explorations using the social change model: Leadership development among college men and women. *Journal of College Student Development, 47*, 217–225. doi: 10.1353/csd.2006.0015

Earl, J., & Kimport, K. (2011). *Digitally enabled social change: Activism in the internet age*. Cambridge, MA: MIT Press.

Evans, M., & Knight Abowitz, K. (Eds.). (2015). *New Directions for Student Leadership: No. 148. Engaging youth in leadership for social and political change*. San Francisco, CA: Jossey-Bass.

Guthrie, K. L., Bertrand Jones, T., & Osteen, L. (2016). *New Directions for Student Leadership: No. 152. Developing culturally relevant leadership learning*. San Francisco, CA: Jossey-Bass.

Metcalf, M., & Barnes, A. (2015). *Innovative leadership workbook for college students*. Tucson, AZ: Integral Publishers.

Nickels, A., Rowland, T., & Fadase, O. (2011). Engaging undergraduate students to be agents of social change: Lessons from student affairs professionals. *Journal of Public Affairs Education, 17*(1). 45–59. Retrieved from: http://www.naspaa.org/JPAEMessenger/Article/VOL17-1/06_17n01_NickelsRowlandFadase.pdf

Owen, J. E. (Ed.). (2015). *New Directions for Student Leadership: No.145. Innovative learning for leadership development*. San Francisco, CA: Jossey-Bass.

Owen, J. E., Komives, S. R., Lucas, N., & McMahon, T. R. (Eds.). (2007). *Instructor's guide for exploring leadership: For college students who want to make a difference.* San Francisco, CA: Jossey-Bass. Available for download at: https://nclp.umd.edu/include/pdfs/publications/exploringleadershipguide.pdf/.

Rath, T., & Conchie, B. (2008). *Strengths based leadership: Great leaders, teams, and why people follow.* New York, NY: Gallup Press.

Roberts, D., & Bailey, K. (Eds.). (2016). *New Directions for Student Leadership: No. 151. Assessing student leadership.* San Francisco, CA: Jossey-Bass.

Shankman, M. L., Allen, S. J., & Haber-Curran, P. (2015). *Emotionally intelligent leadership: Facilitation and activity guide.* San Francisco, CA: Jossey-Bass.

Stenta, D., & McFadden, C. (Ed.). (2015). *New Directions for Student Leadership: No. 147. Developing leadership through recreation and athletics.* San Francisco, CA: Jossey-Bass.

Stroh, D. P. (2015). *Systems thinking for social change: A practical guide to solving complex problems, avoiding unintended consequences, and achieving lasting results.* White River Junction, VT: Chelsea Green Publishing.

Wagner, W., Ostick, D. T., & Associates (2013). *Exploring leadership for college students who want to make a difference: Facilitation and activity guide.* San Francisco, CA: Jossey-Bass.

Wagner, W., & Pigza, J. (Eds.). (2016). *New Directions for Student Leadership: No. 150. Leadership development through service-learning.* San Francisco, CA: Jossey-Bass.

› **Media**

Broken Squares collaboration activity: www.hunter.cuny.edu/socwork/nrcfcpp/pass/learning-circles/five/Brokensquares.pdf

Donate a Photo (mobile app): www.donateaphoto.com

Idealist (website): www.idealist.org

Socialbrite (website): www.socialbrite.org/cause-organizations

SRLS Online (website): thestamp.umd.edu/srls

TED Talk videos about social change: www.ted.com/topics/social+change

Volunteer Match (mobile app and online): www.volunteermatch.org

› Suggested Questions for Discussions or Assignments

- How do you engage and interact with others for change initiatives?
- What strategies have you found helpful in clarifying social issues or purpose statements?
- How have you verbalized or demonstrated our opinions and beliefs about social issues? Are your beliefs or goals as clear to others as they seem to you?
- How do you encourage accountability in yourself and among others for the Change process and, ultimately, the Social Change Model objectives?
- What tools will you use to guide assessments of the initiative's progress and the quality of the change process?

› References

Jost, J. T., & Kay, A. C. (2010). Social justice: History, theory, and research. *Handbook of Social Psychology, 30,* 1122–1165. doi:10.1002/9780470561119.socpsy002030

Daniel T. Ostick serves as the Assistant Director for Student and Staff Development in the Department of Resident Life at the University of Maryland, where he earned his doctorate in College Student Personnel. Previously, he worked in Assessment and as the Coordinator for Leadership Curriculum Development and Academic Partnerships in the Adele H. Stamp Student Union-Center for Campus Life at the University of Maryland. Daniel regularly teaches coursework on leadership theory and global leadership, and has published articles and chapters on the Social Change Model (SCM) of Leadership Development, diversity and leadership, and LGBT issues and leadership.

Kristan Cilente Skendall serves as the Associate Director of the Gemstone Honors Program in the Honors College at the University of Maryland, College Park, where she earned her doctorate in College Student Personnel. Previously, she has worked at Georgetown University, the University of Arizona, and the U.S. Department of Education. Kristan has served as a co-lead facilitator with the LeaderShape Institute, has taught numerous leadership courses, has presented at dozens of national and international conferences, was a member of the Multi-Institutional Study of Leadership Research Team, and served as the coordinator for the National Clearinghouse for Leadership Programs.

Kristan Cilente Skendall serves as the Associate Director of the Gemstone Honors Program, a four-year, interdisciplinary, team research program at the University of Maryland, College Park and is also an Affiliate Assistant Professor in the Department of Counseling, Higher Education, and Special Education in the College of Education. Kristan is a leadership educator who has worked at Georgetown University, the University of Arizona, the U.S. Department of Education, and ACPA-College Student Educators International. Kristan has served as a co-lead facilitator with the Leader-Shape Institute, has taught numerous leadership courses, has presented at dozens of national and international conferences, and was a member of the Multi-Institutional Study of Leadership Research Team. She has served on the executive council of ACPA-College Student Educators International, served as chair of the 2015 ACPA Annual Convention, has been an associate at the National Leadership Symposium, and served as the coordinator for the National Clearinghouse for Leadership Programs (NCLP). Kristan earned her B.A. at the College of William & Mary in sociology and history, her M.A. at the University of Arizona in higher education administration, and her Ph.D. at the University of Maryland in college student personnel.

Daniel T. Ostick is the Assistant Director for Student and Staff Development in the Department of Resident Life at the University of Maryland and is an Affiliate Assistant Professor in the Department of Counseling, Higher Education, and Special Education in the College of Education. Previously, he was the Assistant Director for Assessment, Communication, and Administration and the Coordinator for Leadership Curriculum Development and Academic Partnerships in the Adele H. Stamp Student Union—Center for Campus Life at the University of Maryland, College Park. Daniel has served as a co-lead facilitator with the LeaderShape Institute, regularly teaches coursework on leadership theory and global leadership, and has published articles and chapters on the Social Change Model of Leadership Development, diversity and leadership, and LGBT issues and leadership. He has held positions in residence life at the University of Maryland, the University of Texas at Austin, and the University of Illinois at Urbana-Champaign. Daniel earned his Ph.D. in college student personnel from the University of Maryland, received his master's degree in college student personnel administration from Indiana University, and obtained his undergraduate degree in advertising from the University of Georgia.

Susan R. Komives is Professor Emerita at the University of Maryland. She is past president of the Council for the Advancement of Standards in Higher Education and ACPA-College Student Educators International. She was vice president of two colleges and is the author/editor of a dozen books including *Student Services: A Handbook for the Profession*, *Exploring Leadership*, *Leadership for a Better World*, and the *Handbook for Student Leadership Development*. She is executive founding editor of the New Directions in Student Leadership series. She was a member of the teams that developed *Learning Reconsidered*, the Relational Leadership Model, the Multi-Institutional Study of Leadership, and the Leadership Identity Development grounded theory. She was a member of the Ensemble that developed the Social Change Model of Leadership Development. She is co-founder of the National Clearinghouse for Leadership Programs (NCLP), and a former member of the Board of Directors of the International Leadership Association (ILA). Dr. Komives is a recipient of ACPA and NASPA outstanding research awards, the Distinguished Leadership & Service Award from the Association of Leadership Educators, and the ACPA Lifetime Achievement Award.

Wendy Wagner is the Honey W. Nashman Fellow for Faculty Development in the Honey W. Nashman Center for Civic Engagement and Public Service, and Visiting Assistant Professor of Human Services & Social Justice at The George Washington University. Previously, Wendy served as the Director of the Center for Leadership and Community Engagement, and Assistant

Professor of Leadership and Community Engagement in New Century College at George Mason University. Wendy is a co-editor of *Leadership for a Better World* and *The Handbook for Student Leadership Development*, as well as *Exploring Leadership: For College Students Who Want to Make a Difference: Facilitator Activity Guide* and the accompanying *Student Workbook*. She is also co-editor of *Leadership Development through Service-Learning*, an issue in the New Directions for Student Leadership series. She is a 2010 recipient of the American Association of Colleges & Universities K. Patricia Cross Future Leaders Award.